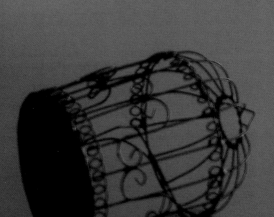

Gene Marshall

GIRL STAR

MEL ODOM

HYPERION

Written by MICHAEL SOMMERS *and* MEL ODOM

Illustrations by CLYDE SMITH *and by* MEL ODOM

Photographs by STEVEN MAYS

Art Direction by BETH TONDREAU ★ *Design by* BTDNYC

Preface

A small child, dressed in pajamas, sits on the floor in front of a large black-and-white television set. It is late. The house is otherwise still and dark, and the child's parents and brother are asleep. With the sound lowered so as not to wake anyone, he sits close enough to the screen to be bathed in its silver-blue light.

His focus has narrowed to this flickering optic window through which a world expands. He has only the vaguest understanding or interest in the mechanical workings of the actual television set. To him TV is another land, and Hollywood, the capital of that land. He has learned of Hollywood by osmosis through contact with his family, friends, and baby-sitter.

It is dreams he is watching and dreaming that he does there with his eyes open, following a particular figure as she glides from scene to scene.

He does not realize that this movie is the previous decade's depiction of the previous century. To him it is now, and vital, and real. Rather than a different time, he thinks it is a different place, a place where the homes and cities and even the unattractive people are all beautiful in their art-directed perfection. But this particular figure he watches seems to be the focal point for everyone's attention.

"It's Gene," he says to himself. He has heard her name from his father, though it will be a while before he realizes that she has a second name of Marshall or, in fact, any last name at all. To him, at present, she is only Gene. She is certainly the most beautiful and captivating face within her silver and celluloid world of many beautiful faces.

Innately he understands that beneath the surface of this gloss is a beating heart and a soul made visible by the odd chemistry that happens once in a blue moon

7

between camera and subject. This chemistry enables him somehow to care for Gene in the same way as millions of other people, and yet feel that she is his alone.

Of course, I was that small boy, and what I described was only the beginning of my lifelong fascination with Gene Marshall. She was my hobby long before I knew what the word "hobby" meant.

Gene Marshall's meteoric rise from nowhere to stardom happened at a time when America needed a story like hers in which to believe. We were a people tired of the postdepression blues and wary of the war breaking out in Europe.

Gene's story of chance, talent, and good fortune, of being in the right place at the right time, was a tonic. It was a sign that great things were still happening for folks and hinted at the possibility that your own lucky break might be just around the corner. Her story caught fire and gave every shop girl, bus driver, housewife, and farmer who listened to the radio or read the news a jolt of grass-green optimism.

Gene's tale of being whisked away to Hollywood for a chance at movie stardom became an emblem of hope for a burgeoning legion of fans who saw her as their stand-in for a shot at the big time. A real-life, real-time story unfolded, and the world got to watch. When the real girl emerged from behind the publicity and hype and proved to be even better than anyone could have hoped for, the public, for once, was given a reality that outclassed the come-on.

Much has been written about Gene's earliest success and much of it is simply not true. The Hollywood press played pretty loose and easy with the facts back then, and studios molded the truth to fit their needs. So in an effort to set the records straight, I have made it my lifelong quest to collect and assemble the facts of Gene Marshall's story from the paper trail of publicity that chronicled her public life, and from the personal recollections of people who were there and actually saw her life unfold. As one of her more devoted fans, I have made it my business to collect interviews from both the printed and recorded sources, as well as conduct my own whenever possible.

GENE MARSHALL carved images on film that elicit unsurpassed cinematic worship, especially in the movies when directed by her mentor-Svengali, Erik von Sternberg.

Her earliest film with Von Sternberg, *Blonde Lace,* blazed a trail to the noir side still traveled today by filmmakers. A movie that rolled with the punches and evolved from a light comedy into a dark tale of moral and literal shadow and light, *Blonde Lace* was a valentine dipped in poison, with Gene as the flower trapped inside.

The flower girl, Marjorie, was the first in a series of wildly varied roles that established Gene as one of the most versatile and poetic actresses of her generation.

But how did she go so far so fast, and what did she have to pay to get there? How does a teenage girl, regardless of how beautiful and resourceful, go from high school plays to star billing at Monolithic Pictures in less than a year?

This book is an attempt to answer these questions and explain the dynamics involved in the rise of a star.

From magazine and newspaper clippings, radio broadcast transcripts, and letters and documents loaned to me or purchased through estate sales and auction houses, I have assembled enough evidence to give a good idea of what took place.

After reading her amazing book *The Way We Wore*, I contacted the charming and articulate Marsha Hunt. Miss Hunt has been that rare phenomenon, a beautiful leading lady capable of character roles since her teen years at Paramount Pictures from the late 1930s to the present.

She not only set me straight on some pertinent Hollywood facts, but also recalled her own brief and telling meeting with Gene during her earliest approach to stardom.

Frank DeCaro, scribe and media commentator for, among others, the *New York Times*, graciously allowed me to print a portion of an unpublished interview that he recorded with the elusive Miss Marshall. My gratitude is exceeded only by my envy at his having met her.

All interviews are ones that I myself have conducted unless otherwise stated.

Together with my collection of interviews and quotes from previously published materials, I have written down the fairy tale as I believe it actually happened.

Miss Marshall, herself, living in Italy for many years, has given her blessing to this project. I would not have proceeded otherwise. Famously reclusive, she would not agree to be interviewed for this book, but she did very generously contact many of her friends and fellow performers and told them they could speak to me freely and honestly without any fear of her displeasure. I will remain forever in her debt.

—MEL ODOM

Contents

for
MARIANNE CLARKSON
and
GENE BAGNATO

Gene Marshall

GIRL STAR

Cora Harper

1

Discovery

CORA HARPER

Transcription from *Non-Stop Hollywood* radio broadcast (February 17, 1941)

--Yes—Yes—Hand me the microphone, Tommy.... (inaudible) I don't care a hill of beans about the sponsor. Forget him! This is news! This is the biggest—They'll all thank me for it later! Are we on? (inaudible) You go down there and find out ... oh, we are on!

--Hello, America, from Hollywood on the Hudson, New York City, U.S. of A. It's your very own Cora Harper with <u>Non-Stop</u> <u>Hollywood</u>. Brought to you in a coast-to-coast broadcast from the Regency Theater in Times Square.

--Right this instant, Hollywood history is being made in a miraculous chain of events.

--Just moments ago, a beautiful young girl was led out of the auditorium where "Deep Devotion" is having its gala East Coast premiere. Monolithic Pictures' latest million-dollar release, starring Madra Lord and Trent Osborn! The premiere is still going on, in fact—

--But no one cares! Well, perhaps Madra Lord does—big time!—

--But this beautiful girl—

--I can't tell you how ravishing—

--She's an usherette here at the Regency.

--Only a few minutes ago, she was simply doing her little job. Escorting Erik von Sternberg to his seat. You see, the celebrated movie director was arriving late for the debut of his own picture! But that's typical. The great Von Sternberg makes his own time! Anyway, the movie had already begun and—

--This little usherette, flashlight in hand, was guiding the fabled director to his place in the darkened theater crammed with cinema celebrities and society swells—oh, they're all here—Brenda Frazier, Billy Rose, Tallulah, Robert Sherwood, Mark Hellinger, and Gladys Glad—

--But now, every eye is focused upon her. This girl!

--This startled babe in the woods has suddenly been thrust into the glare of the brightest lights Hollywood can possibly shine on its gods and goddesses.

--She has been discovered! Discovered like I haven't seen in all my years of covering Hollywood. Taken by the hand of the great Von Sternberg himself and swept into the lobby here, where he is proclaiming her as his newest and most astonishing find.

--Yours truly has never witnessed such commotion over an unknown. From my vantage place on the grand staircase of the Regency, I can barely see this girl as she stands in a cluster of photographers. Can't you hear the flashbulbs going off?

--She's there on Von Sternberg's arm. He's keeping the photographers at bay with the help of some ushers and, yes, a policeman. There's absolute pandemonium. People are streaming out of the auditorium to get a look at what's going on out here—

--Getting a look at her!

--Let me tell you, she's—a honey blonde. The biggest ice-water-blue eyes you ever saw. Tall and graceful. Classy, like a debutante. And, oh, such a sweet face.

--Heavens, I've seen stars come and I've seen them go in my time. Clara Bow and Nancy Carroll and Harold Lloyd and—I interviewed Garbo before she could speak English! But I tell you in all honesty, I've never seen anything like—

--Why, I don't know her name yet. My assistant Tommy is trying to find out. He's somewhere down there in the crowd.

--Little old me, I was upstairs in the manager's office when all this excitement began, going over my notes for this broadcast. I previewed the picture yesterday. You'll read what I think about "Deep Devotion" in my syndicated newspaper column tomorrow. It's a little slow in places, but it's Madra Lord at her dreamiest and you know how wonderful she can be.

--Now a squad car just pulled up in front of the theater with policemen to hold back the mob. The lobby is thronged with hundreds of people and more coming every second.... (inaudible) What? No, that's impossible—they didn't! I'm told they've stopped the film. Just stopped it cold in mid-premiere! Why, I never—

--Heavens, there goes Madra Lord. Looking like death on a cracker. Fighting her way through the crowd. Not a single person seems to even notice she's there. Or cares. Why, I do believe she's walking out on her own premiere!

--Well, I guess this isn't Madra's premiere anymore! It's suddenly all about this unknown little girl.

--I would think that all those constant camera flashes must be positively blinding down there—everything is reflecting off the walls of mirrors lining the lobby. It doesn't seem to be troubling the girl, though....

--Now Von Sternberg has maneuvered his discovery over by the concessions counter so that she's not completely surrounded by photographers. Her little pillbox hat has been knocked sideways and—oh, Von Sternberg just straightened it back on her head. That's the director's trademark, you know, absolute perfection!

--Now wait a minute! Madra Lord didn't leave the theater after all. There she is, pushing her way past the press. Joining Von Sternberg and his protégée. She's kissing him and putting her arm around the girl. Whispering something in her ear. Well, isn't that grand! That Madra is being such a trouper, helping to buck up that poor bewildered child! What a pro she is!

--I can't begin to tell you how thrilling ... (inaudible) What did you say, Tommy? June? Jane? Wait—I've just been given the mystery girl's name. It's—it's—

--I'm telling you, ladies and gentlemen, if tonight's excitement is any indication, if stars really can be born overnight, tomorrow all of America will be asking—WHO IS GENE MARSHALL?

--Well, you heard it here first. From me, your very own Cora Harper. On Non-Stop Hollywood.

2

Early Years

KATHRYN GENE MARSHALL WAS BORN IN 1923 IN COS COB,
CONNECTICUT, WHERE SHE GREW UP AS THE SECOND CHILD
OF DR. ALFRED MARSHALL AND HIS WIFE ALICE.

The following extracts are from archived interviews conducted for a February 17, 1951,
Time magazine cover story on Gene Marshall.

DR. STERLING ROGERS
Family physician

Prettiest baby I ever delivered. Those big blue eyes just opened up and took in the
whole wide world as calmly as you'd please. Of course, babies don't see right away,
but this one sure looked as if she did.

Lord knows nobody ever wanted a baby girl more than Alice and Alf Marshall.
After their boy Alexander—Sandy—was born, they had to wait almost ten years before Katie came along.

Kathryn Gene Marshall. They'd had that name already picked out for I don't
know how long. She was named for Alice's mother and Alf's father Eugene. She was
Katie the whole time she lived here in Cos Cob. She didn't switch her name to Gene
till she moved to Hollywood, I suppose.

Both the Marshall children were healthy kids. Alf firmly believed in an apple a
day and plenty of sunshine and sleep for his kids, and they thrived on it. Beautiful
children. Poor Sandy was one of the handsomest young men you'd ever see, and as
for Katie—well, she became a movie star, didn't she?

VIOLA VINSON
Neighbor

My, but that Katie was one sweet child. Doc Marshall and Alice would get me to baby-sit her, just as I did for her brother Sandy when he was little.

When Katie smiled, she looked like the happiest kiddie on earth. Right off a jar of baby food. When she wasn't smiling, though, Katie would get this other expression. Like she could see right through you. Like she knew what you were thinking.

I was the only sitter Katie ever had besides her brother. We'd cut out paper dolls. She just loved them. I remember she always wanted me to cut out each individual finger on their hands. Insisted that it had to be done that way.

Such a fanciful little thing. Always seeing fairies and elves. Got me half believing in them myself. One time, Katie must have been about five, she threw the neighborhood in a tizzy when she got all the other kids to help her hunt pixies in the field behind the First Presbyterian Church. Dinnertime came and nobody knew where their children were. You never saw such carrying on until we found them.

That child. What an active imagination. Had trouble sleeping, though. Sometimes I'd have to sit up with Katie when she was put to bed. She hated being alone in the dark. Even with a night light, she'd be scared. I'd try to explain to her that there were no such things as ghosts. But if you can believe in fairies, ghosts just seem logical, I suppose.

IRENE RINKS
Neighbor

I don't know where Katie got the bumble-bee costume. Was it an old recital outfit she found somewhere? Her mother probably had a fit over Katie digging in people's trash. Anyway, Katie found this bee get-up. Yellow, with stripes and wings made of blue gauze. Well, that child all but lived in it one summer. Ran all around the neighborhood. Buzz, buzz, buzz. She was so cute. Going into people's gardens and telling them she was a bee.

VIOLA VINSON

Sandy Marshall was one of the finest boys you'd ever hope to meet. We all thought he was going to grow up to be president of the United States.

You should have seen him with Katie. Sandy was ten years old when she was born, and boys usually aren't good with babies, you know. But from the day Katie arrived, she was a little princess as far as he was concerned.

Pushed her around in her carriage. Read to her. Everything. Sandy taught Katie to swim, and how to ride a bike, and even how to play croquet. And he must have taken a million pictures of her with his Kodak Brownie while she was growing up.

And, well, naturally Katie thought that he was a prince. A big handsome older brother like that? Of course.

IRENE RINKS

Girls were crazy for Sandy. But you better believe they had to pass muster with little Katie before he'd go out with any of them.

My Evelyn was only a year or so younger than Sandy, and they knew each other forever. But the only time I think I ever saw Katie lose her temper was at a picnic when Evelyn hung on to Sandy's arm too long. Threw a tantrum right there.

A pair, those two. Inseparable. I'd see them from my kitchen window—that tall blond teenage boy and his kid sister. All those long summer afternoons together, playing croquet in their backyard. Sandy won scholarships to colleges all over, but he chose Yale so he'd be near to home.

You should have seen how proud Sandy looked when Katie played Cinderella in her school play. She was quite the little actress even then. Oh, that scene when Katie tried on the glass slipper!

Sandy Marshall

DR. STERLING ROGERS

I don't know what the Marshalls would have done after Sandy died if they didn't have Katie to help them get through it. It was agony for them, losing him. Somehow Katie took it like a soldier and managed to keep them going.

IRENE RINKS

Sandy was a sophomore at Yale when it happened, so Katie must have been nine or ten. Normally, Sandy took the train when he'd come home for a visit, but someone offered him a lift for the Thanksgiving holidays. They barely got out of New Haven. The other car's fault, they say. Both boys were killed instantly.

Katie came to my kitchen door. It was early evening. The night before Thanksgiving. I remember I was just setting out my pumpkin pies to cool. She told me that Sandy had been in a car crash and was dead. She asked me would I come sit with her mother.

Katie just sat in a corner, holding her teddy bear, while poor Alice cried on and on. Not Katie, though. Not a tear. But I hope I never again see such a stricken look on a child's face.

VIOLA VINSON

Time doesn't heal everything, but sorrow does get easier with time. Eventually, life returned to normal, more or less, for the Marshalls. But it was always a quiet house

after that. The doctor was busy with his practice while Alice threw herself into volunteer work with the church. As for Katie, well, whatever time she had left after school and such, she'd spend it going to the movies.

IRENE RINKS

Boys? Oh, certainly, once Katie got into her teens, there were boys. Plenty. She just didn't have time for them. Play practice at school kept her busy, and she went to the pictures a lot. Crazy about the pictures, even then. Did you know that?

My Evelyn was keen on going to the pictures, too. But it was different somehow with Katie. Sometimes I'd go with her, and it was like she was in church. Those big blue eyes would get bigger, and she'd sit there drinking it all in. *A Star Is Born, 100 Men and a Girl,* and *Stage Door* were ones she saw over and over again—dragged everyone she knew to see them with her. Spent all of her allowance on those pictures.

KATHRYN GENE MARSHALL
DRAMA CLUB, MOVIE CLUB
FUTURE: BLUE SKIES FOR BLUE EYES

Cos Cob High School senior portrait, 1940

DR. STERLING ROGERS

Oh, I have a little story for you. Katie came to see me one day in the late thirties. Said it was private. Asked me what it was like to have a baby. I said, "Do you think you're going to have one?" You can imagine. Katie laughed and said no, but she needed to know in case she got a chance to audition for the part of Scarlett in *Gone With the Wind.* Seems she had sent her photo to Hollywood and was sure that they were going to test her for it. Having a baby was part of the movie, she said.

DOROTHY SAMMS
Cos Cob High School English teacher

Katie was active in our drama club. She played Juliet and Yum-Yum for us. I suppose she was all right. Nothing outstanding, or I'd remember more.

Boys flocked around her but there was no one particular boy she liked. Katie was sweet but rather shy. "Preoccupied" might be a better term. Back then, I imagine that Katie saw boys as something convenient to have around. They'd take her to the movies.

VIOLA VINSON

If Doctor and Alice had their way, Katie would have stayed at home with them forever. But Katie had a mind of her own, you know. Soon as she graduated from high school, she started pestering them about going to New York. No college for her, no sir. She had those eyes of hers set on something else.

3

Before the Dawn

CAROLINE RICHMOND TODD
Former Manhattan roommate

They don't have residential hotels for women anymore, do they? Not like the Barbizon, at any rate. Some places for girls like the Three Arts Club were dumpy brownstones, but the Barbizon was a first-class establishment. It was such a beautiful place to live that it didn't much matter how strict the rules were about comings and goings.

No men allowed upstairs, of course. I remember Dr. Marshall being miffed when he couldn't see Gene's room. "But I'm her daddy," he kept telling the clerks, who of course had heard the same argument a million times over.

I was studying to be a fashion illustrator. Can you imagine what it's like to have a beauty like Gene as a roommate when you're an artist? I drew her constantly. Years later, long after I gave up my career to marry Mr. Todd and have a family, I held an exhibition at the country club here that included three crayon portraits I did of Gene.

The prices people offered were astounding. No, I didn't sell, much as I was tempted to. I still keep them as a souvenir of the six months I shared a room with Gene. Not many people can say they lived with a legend waiting to happen.

Gene was friendly but quiet. "Contemplative." Mad for the movies. The first thing Gene did was get herself a night job ushering at the Regency Theater so she could see the movies for free. You'd think that watching the same movie over and over again would be a bore, but Gene liked it. Said it gave her the chance to study them.

Even when Gene started getting modeling work, she hung on to her Regency job. She didn't want to ask her parents for money. Dating? Where would she have found time?

FREDERICK CHAMBERS
Founder of Chambers Model Agency

We signed her on the spot. As I recall, Gene was exceptionally poised for a seventeen-year-old novice. She came to see us with her mother, who turned out to be the excitable one. The mother practically fainted when I said yes, we'd give Gene a contract.

Actually, there was a bit of a to-do over her contract. Gene said she wouldn't do certain sorts of modeling. No cigarettes, no lingerie, no liquor ads. That's unusual, but I liked that. Showed class.

Gene landed a few good assignments with us, but not as many as one might suppose. How do I put this? In terms of her appearance, Gene was more of an orchid back in a day when daisies were in style. She was a little too exotic looking for most of my clientele. Not actually exotic, mind you. Just exotic looking.

One of the first places I sent Gene was *DeLuxe* magazine. She was just their type.

★ In 1987, the doors of the Chambers Model Agency were finally shut, a casualty of the escalating "Model Wars." Among discarded items were several folders of photos from models' portfolios no longer current. These pages from Gene Marshall's 1940–41 portfolio were among them.

My sincere thanks to Carol Navin, who had worked at Chambers and called me saying she had "some pictures you might like." —Mel

De Luxe

GENE MARSHALL
SPRING'S
FRESHEST
FACE

APRIL 1941
Price 35 cents
40 cents in Canada

CARMEL DE LORIAN
Editor emeritus, *DeLuxe* magazine

The first time Gene Marshall walked into our office, we all just sat there and stared, thinking, *THIS* is what being eighteen is all about. I'm sure our mouths were *WIDE* open. She was an absolute *BABY,* right out of high school.

But refined. White gloves. Never a hair out of place. Such an exquisite package, with this nice, sweet, *GENUINE* girl inside.

We used Gene twice right away, and she was *DIVINE.* Green, but really, that's to be expected.

Gene had this innate poise. Something they can't teach you. She still has it today, more than ever. Back then, she'd stand in front of the camera, listen to the photographer's directions, and then off she'd go into this serene place inside herself somewhere. And suddenly, there'd be the image we wanted.

Oh, we *SIMPLY* ate her up, breakfast, lunch, and dinner. We'd have used her a lot more, but Dame Fortune had other plans for our little Gene, didn't she?

When she hit so fast in Hollywood that first year, we went through all the photos from her sessions and pulled one for a spring cover. *FANTASTIC* reader reaction. It became one of our biggest sellers.

EDGAR MERRYWEATHER
Former manager of the Regency Theater

I'm proud of the fact that a number of the Regency's corps of ushers eventually became stars themselves. None of the boys ever did, strangely enough, except for Tennessee Williams, this oddball Southern fellow who turned into the playwright a few years later. But among our usherettes over the years, we employed Lucille Ball, Lizbeth Scott, and most famous of them all, Gene Marshall. She was with us for nearly half a year, in the winter of 1940.

Now, I've known a zillion movie fans in my day, but Gene was special. After seating the audience, she'd always watch whatever film was showing. No matter how many times she'd seen it before. Rapt. Practically hypnotized. One time I had to speak to Gene sternly about getting too involved in the screen when she should be attending to the customers. Only once, though. She was very conscientious.

That night in February when Gene was discovered by Erik von Sternberg is one of the most famous in the Regency's seventy-year history. When they finish that awful hotel they're building in its place, I almost think they should put up a plaque marking the spot. Every one of her Monolithic releases premiered at the Regency. Whenever Gene came back for them, she always used to linger a moment by her old usherette's station.

STEWART BUSCH

From *Maharajah of the Movies: Reuben Lilienthal and the Cult of the Studio Chief* (New York: Eaker & MacKay, 1973)

As 1941 began, Reuben Lilienthal was secretly worried that Monolithic's might was waning. The studio had cleared only a marginal profit in 1940, and revenues were lagging for nearly the first time in Monolithic's twenty-year history.

Lilienthal was concerned about the future. As the lucrative European market was curtailed by the war abroad, he wondered what America's probable entry into the conflict would bode for the film industry.

He judged that the American public would favor escapist fare during a time of war. Musicals, stylish romances, tricky detective sagas, he reckoned, perhaps the occasional patriotic action film. "No scripts with a message," he instructed the Writing Department in a January 15 memo. "If we need a message, we'll call Western Union."

Lilienthal, however, also faced more immediate challenges. His five-year campaign to upgrade the studio lot had achieved wonders, but funds to complete the project were scarce. Lilienthal had bullied his board of directors into securing outside financing, but bankers were reluctant to provide more. They wanted some of the outstanding debt repaid.

Prowling his domain, Lilienthal didn't like seeing the cluster of rickety wooden structures from the studio's silent days huddling like poor relations near his shining new soundstages. They reminded the mogul too much of his early struggles. But he was forced to postpone replacing them until the financial picture brightened.

Relief looked unlikely. The studio's fall releases had not performed to expectations. The budget overruns on the recently completed *Deep Devotion* were modest compared to the skyrocketing costs of *Blonde Lace,* which had begun shooting in late January. Erik von Sternberg, usually a methodical director, was inexplicably wasting countless hours and film to shoot the simplest of scenes. Von Sternberg seemed to have lost his creative drive, miring himself in details and despondent behavior.

Madra Lord, once merely a moneymaking annoyance, had grown ever more temperamental with continued success. Nominated for an Academy Award for *He Married His Boss,* Lord no longer bothered to confine her tantrums to the studio lot. Lilienthal instructed the head of the publicity department to assign a representative to be near the actress no matter where she went.

Harry Hale balked. "Not everywhere?" he questioned.

"I don't care if she's going to the ladies' room at Bullock's Department Store," snapped Lilienthal, "I want somebody with Madra at all times in case she goes nuts!"

All they needed was a scandal. "I can just see Madra running over some poor little match girl on the corner of Sunset and Vine," muttered Lilienthal.

After reviewing his roster of female stars, Lilienthal ordered extensive talent searches. Lord was the most popular among Monolithic's half dozen leading ladies, but she was generally limited to serious emotional roles. Rising Ivy Jordan was funny, but her sarcastic edge wasn't right for romance. The others were capable and attractive actresses, but Lilienthal found them somehow lacking in magnetism. His overtures to Paulette Goddard and Linda Darnell to join the studio foundered in contract negotiations.

Watching the rushes, Lilienthal scanned the crowd scenes. Whenever he saw a fresh face who might brighten a thousand marquees, tests were made. But his elusive dream girl continued to evade discovery.

From all appearances, the Monolithic assembly line smoothly churned out its attractions: one new feature every ten days, short subjects and cartoons every other day. But within its grand walls, the studio's boss knew all too well that his dream machine was built upon a thin layer of other people's money. One good yank from the bankers, and the entire operation could go down like a house of cards.

On the eve of his fiftieth birthday, in February, Lilienthal was occupied with re-cutting *Breakfast in Bed* to the censors' satisfaction. Unable to attend the New York opening of *Deep Devotion,* instead he sent Monolithic names to lend glamour to the premiere. To do so, he briefly halted production on *Blonde Lace,* hoping that a hiatus might improve the director's faltering grasp on the feature.

Instead, Von Sternberg made the discovery Lilienthal had dreamed about.

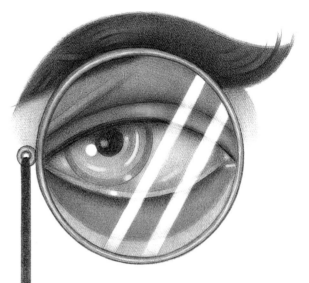

4

Premiere

Erik von Sternberg
From his autobiography, *Eye for Beauty*
(New York: Promethean Press, 1966)

Popcorn.

It is ironic that something so commonplace, so cheap and so banal, in fact, as the scent of popcorn is forever linked in my mind with the wondrous night I first encountered Gene Marshall.

The enchantress. The eternal one.

A quarter of a century since my first glimpse of Gene—and ten years, alas, since we last saw one another—it is a rare interviewer who still does not ask me to describe our meeting. Unwilling to squander one of my finest hours upon some scribbling stranger, I usually say, "That was a lifetime ago. Who can remember?"

But I cannot ever forget.

Scent is the strongest of the senses, and for me, oddly, Gene Marshall's discovery will always be associated with an overpowering smell of popcorn.

She and I stood together in the mirrored lobby of the theater, having our pictures taken again and again by dozens of photographers, with countless others standing as close as they could to prove they were there. I closed my eyes now and again to rest them between the camera flashes, trying to be alone in my moment of discovery.

Savoring it.

Who this beautiful child might become had scarcely begun to reveal itself to me. At the center of a huge commotion—shouting newsmen, shrieking movie fans, celebrities desperate to share her magic—Gene Marshall was the calm eye of a whirling storm. An oasis of poised loveliness in the midst of chaos.

Standing next to her, with my eyes closed, scent and sound merged as one. I usually shun publicity for myself and am not one to have my photo taken. Even with my eyes shut, all was red. In my ears, a cacophonous din of voices, sirens, flashbulb pops, footsteps on tile, rustling fabric, yes, even the pounding of my heart.

And there was that fragrance of popcorn—that smell of an audience hungry for dreams.

Gene Marshall possesses the blue eyes of my mother's family. Eyes similar to my own. That night, when I first saw her, when I first looked deeply into Gene's eyes within the slim beam of her usher's flashlight, I felt a mystical sensation of reflection. A sense of oneness. A mystical notion that Gene's eyes were mirroring my own gave me in that instant a vision of her future expanding and bonding with mine.

Her newness was intoxicating, and I urgently wished for Gene to have a wonderful career and existence, so that in my selfishness I could live it vicariously through her.

She would be my female self.

TRENT OSBORN

From his unpublished memoir, *My Bed of Roses* [circa 1975]

(Courtesy of La Jolla University's Film and Theater Archives)

Deep Devotion took forever. Always a taskmaster, Erik had never been so rigorous. Countless take after take. Nothing satisfied. Hours of getting the light just so on Madra's face. Making the curl of smoke from my cigarette drift exactly in a certain direction. It was agony going over the same motions again and again to conform with whatever impossible idea of perfection Erik was trying to achieve.

I felt like a robot. Exhausted by the end of each day, the shooting affected my social life drastically, finishing off my romances with Ginger and Bette.

I thought I'd go nuts when RL told me that we'd reteam for *Blonde Lace*. I didn't know which was worse: Madra's fire or Erik's ice. I knew that making another movie with those two maniacs was punishment for the Lana Turner incident, but RL said I had no choice and, besides, playing a cynical detective would contrast with the chump I was in *Deep Devotion*.

It felt like we began making the new movie before we finished with the other. Erik was being even more of a perfectionist, too. Nothing pleased him, from the lapels of my trench coat to the new caps on Madra's teeth. Shooting crawled along. One endless day, Madra and I did thirty-three takes to get a simple "hello" shot done to Erik's satisfaction. After one week of filming, we had managed to get only a few minutes in the can.

That's why RL shut down *Blonde Lace* and sent us all to New York. Erik didn't want to go to the premiere, but RL closed the picture right from under him.

Deep Devotion premiered at the Regency, Monolithic's flagship house. RL built it in the late twenties after Monolithic beat every other studio to the punch in making talking pictures. Suddenly lousy with money, the Regency was RL's way to show the industry that Monolithic was in business for keeps. It's a Times Square grind house now, but in 1941, the Regency was a showplace. The lobby was based on the Hall of Mirrors from Versailles, only bigger. Armies of ushers in pale blue uniforms.

It was the usual premiere hoopla. Madra was between husbands then, so I escorted her. We had cocktails and a few laughs before going. Madra was in a good mood that night, looking every inch a star in the same gold dress she wore in the

movie's Monte Carlo scene. We'd screened *Deep Devotion* before leaving the coast and thought it was swell. Reaction to the sneak previews had been fine, too, so everything was going along swimmingly.

A huge crush of fans, photographers, and newsreel men greeted us. As usual, a few girls got past the police and tore my new dinner jacket. Anyway, we did our gracious blah-blahs for the press. Madra was annoyed when Erik couldn't be found. But she smiled graciously in every direction as we swept past all the mirrors and into the theater.

Seats some rows behind us were vacant. Erik's seats. "That Kraut better show up PDQ," muttered Madra just as the lights went down.

IVY JORDAN

Really, I don't recall how I wound up at the premiere. I was billed, what, fifth or sixth down in the credits? Wisecracks and a drunk scene with Madra, that's all my part was. Because I was doing *Blonde Lace,* too, somehow I got included on the trip. Erik liked having me around, I think. Anyway, I went along for the joy ride. Figured I could take in a couple of shows and blow some dough at Hattie Carnegie's. See what was going on down at Sammy's in the Bowery as well as uptown at "21," you know?

Well, it's a long time ago, so I can mention there was a certain gent in New York I was anxious to spend time with. He came with me to the premiere. Nobody made much fuss over me, so we were in our seats for Madra's grand entrance. Oh, you should have seen her sail down the aisle. Slinky gold lamé and miles of mink, and poor Trent pulled along in her wake like a sailboat behind an ocean liner.

Anyway, the picture scarcely gets underway when Erik arrives. The usher is showing him to his seat, right next to us, when suddenly Erik snatches the usher's flashlight and shines it directly into her face.

Gene Marshall's face. Like no other face in the world.

In two seconds flat, Erik grabs this girl by the arm and all but throws her over into the empty seat between us.

Tell me, Mel, how old are you? You realize, of course, that Gene was established in the public's collective conscious long before you hit this planet. So you grew up with her. You have no idea what encountering her for the very first time was like. Especially from only a few inches away. Listen to me, kiddo: You would have fallen into those blue eyes of hers and drowned.

She knocked Erik sideways to Sunday, that's for sure. Sparks all but flew from his ears. "Let me look at you," he cries, telling her not to get up. "Sit here and watch the film!"

Which is exactly what Gene did, believe it or not. She turned away from him and gazed up at the screen as Madra broke the bank at Monte Carlo or something. Let me tell you, that gal knew how to take direction from the start. She forgot all about Erik and me staring and just lost herself in that silly movie.

Maybe five minutes later, Erik says, "Enough. You're my angel. You're coming with me," and hauls the poor kid up the aisle. I grab my purse and race after them. I wasn't going to miss this. Within seconds of hitting the lobby, flashbulbs start exploding. Boom, boom, boom.

Trent Osborn
From *My Bed of Roses*

Madra knew something was up. There'd been this sudden fuss behind us shortly after the movie began. I tried to get a look, but Madra elbowed me hard in the ribs. Then I heard Erik's unmistakable accent. He said, "You are going to be my angel." At that point, Madra half turned only to see Erik and some people running up the aisle. What could she do? She went back to watching herself.

The Regency was huge, and we were seated perhaps two-thirds of the way down toward the screen. After a while, I could hear others behind us walking out. People in front kept turning around to see what was happening. Every so often, the doors toward the rear of the auditorium would be held open a few seconds and you could hear the sound of voices back there increasing in volume.

What could it be? This commotion evidently wasn't about our picture, which, by the way, looked perfectly fine. Was it about the war in Europe? A catastrophe in Times Square?

In the silver light from the screen, I saw Madra had turned dead white. She was trying to look composed in case anyone was watching, but I could see beads of perspiration breaking out on her forehead. Now people in the rows in front of us were leaving.

"Something's wrong," I whispered.

"Everything is perfectly fine," said Madra through clenched teeth.

Suddenly the picture flickered out and we sat there in darkness.

Madra rose. "He better be good and dead when I get out there."

Difficult as Madra was, you can't blame her for being furious. After all, this was meant to be her triumph. She'd worked like a dog on *Deep Devotion* and gave a swell performance, too. One of her best. And just as the opening credits get rolling, and

Opposite Page: Erik von Sternberg

the whole world is about to get a load of Madra Lord acting up a storm, out of nowhere something upstages her. Totally takes away all the attention.

Madra was ready to kill. Probably capable of it, too, but instead a thousand people watched her be gracious to Gene Marshall out in the lobby. That act was a better performance than anything Madra ever pulled off on-screen.

HARRY HALE, Former Publicity Director for Monolithic Pictures
From The American Screen Foundation's Oral History Project, 1982

It's legend now that we deliberately stopped the film. That Erik or I ordered it.

What happened, I found out later, was that the operators up in the projection booth heard the rumpus rising from the lobby and sneaked out for a peek. So through someone's carelessness there was nobody in the booth to sync the second reel of the movie—projection wasn't automatic in those days, you know. And the film simply ran out. By the time they got it started again, practically everyone was out in the lobby getting a gander at Gene.

ERIK VON STERNBERG
From *Eye for Beauty*

Details. The world always craves more.

They say the power of my best films is in the details.

Perhaps I am being quixotic in not revealing details of that night.

How I was late to the premiere because I could not bear to sit through *Deep Devotion* again. It was a trivial, if amusing, film. I was also displeased with the central performance by Madra Lord. An expert actress, an attractive woman, and a star in her own right, yes, but one with scant creative sympathy. As professionals, we tried to establish a rapport through the making of our several films, but I felt drained by giving Madra the benefit of my direction. She took—and took—but she rarely gave me what I wanted in return.

It was often the same with other stars. They shone, they shimmered, but their light never reflected my soul.

So I arrived at the Regency late, fearing that the world would detect the painful emptiness I felt as a creator. Fearful that *Deep Devotion* would register laughably as a void on celluloid.

So downcast was I that I barely noticed how the theater manager summoned an usherette to conduct me to my seat. As we entered the auditorium, I stumbled in the sudden blackness. The usherette reassuringly gave me her hand.

I felt warmth. Softness. And yet an odd sense of strength, too. I looked up and caught a glimpse of an enchanting face.

MADRA LORD
From her autobiography, *Dark Radiance*
(Toronto: Brown, Brown & Brown, 1978)
Among all my premieres, one of the most exciting was *Deep Devotion*.

The night before, Erik came to my hotel suite and asked a favor.

"Anything you want, my darling," I replied.

"Well," he said, "there is a young girl—an unknown—who I wish to cast in a tiny part in our new picture. Her name is Gene Marshall, and I believe she is very promising."

He showed me a photograph of a pretty blonde youngster. "She's ravishing," I enthused. "If she can act half as well as she looks, she is going to be a star."

Erik proposed to dress the girl as a theater usher and "discover" her in the lobby before the film began. With the press corps covering the premiere, Erik felt that she would garner maximum publicity. But he wanted to make certain that I wouldn't mind sharing my spotlight.

"Not at all," I said, proposing an even more dramatic turn of events. I suggested that Erik should arrive late at the theater and make his great discovery shortly after *Deep Devotion* began. That way, I explained, the press would not be distracted by my presence or by other celebrities in the lobby and could focus their full attention on Erik's new find.

Our little scheme came off beautifully. I will never forget the sweet uproar in the lobby afterward as we all posed together with Erik's new discovery for the press. "You must get used to this, my dear," I whispered to a bedazzled Gene. "You are going to be very, very famous."

OLIVE WILKERSON
From *Metropolitan* magazine,
"Good-bye to Glamour:
Regency Theater Razed"
(June 12, 1998)
"All those years of premieres blur in my head," said former powder room attendant Olive Wilkerson. "But boy, I'll never forget that night back in the early forties when they discovered Gene Marshall. Picked her right out of a line of identically-dressed usherettes.

"All this sudden ruckus outside in the lobby.

Then Miss Madra Lord slams into the powder room, looking ready to kill. She picks up a bottle of Evening in Paris and throws it against the nearest mirror. As hard as she could. Smashed the per-fume, the mirror, everything. Scared me out of a year's growth.

"Then she says, calm as you please, 'Oops,' and walks out.

"Didn't leave me a nickel to clean up after her mess, either."

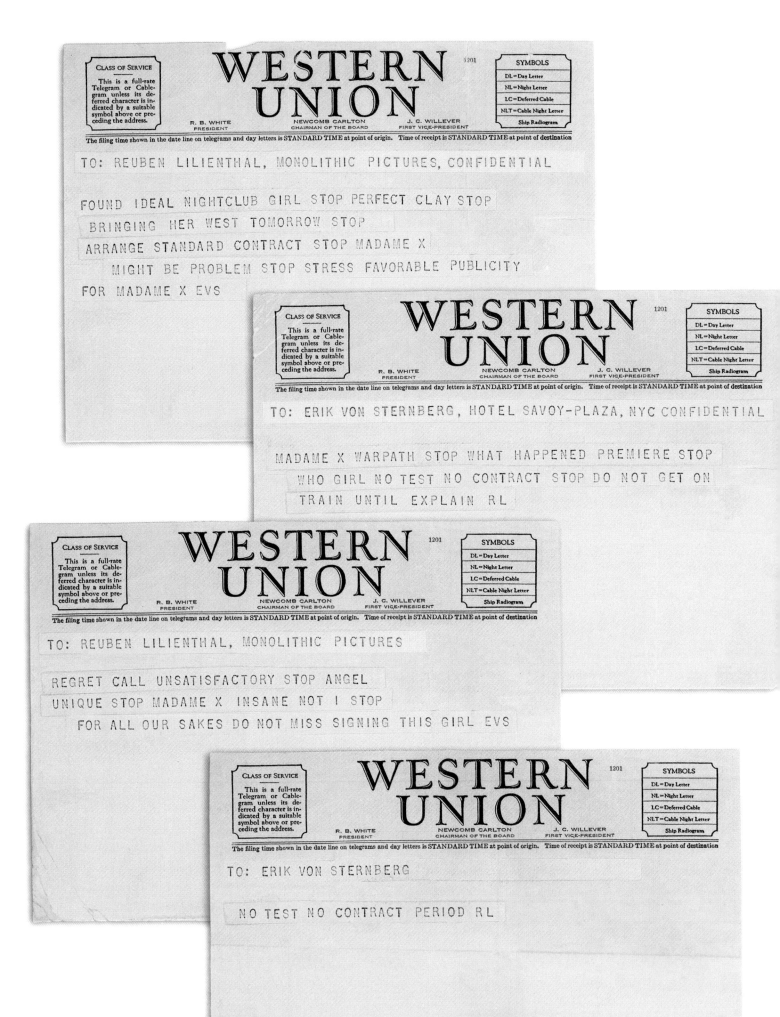

WESTERN UNION 1201

CLASS OF SERVICE
This is a full-rate Telegram or Cablegram unless its deferred character is indicated by a suitable symbol above or preceding the address.

R. B. WHITE PRESIDENT
NEWCOMB CARLTON CHAIRMAN OF THE BOARD
J. C. WILLEVER FIRST VICE-PRESIDENT

SYMBOLS
DL = Day Letter
NL = Night Letter
LC = Deferred Cable
NLT = Cable Night Letter
Ship Radiogram

The filing time shown in the date line on telegrams and day letters is STANDARD TIME at point of origin. Time of receipt is STANDARD TIME at point of destination

TO: REUBEN LILIENTHAL, MONOLITHIC PICTURES, CONFIDENTIAL

FOUND IDEAL NIGHTCLUB GIRL STOP PERFECT CLAY STOP

BRINGING HER WEST TOMORROW STOP

ARRANGE STANDARD CONTRACT STOP MADAME X

MIGHT BE PROBLEM STOP STRESS FAVORABLE PUBLICITY

FOR MADAME X EVS

WESTERN UNION 1201

CLASS OF SERVICE
This is a full-rate Telegram or Cablegram unless its deferred character is indicated by a suitable symbol above or preceding the address.

R. B. WHITE PRESIDENT
NEWCOMB CARLTON CHAIRMAN OF THE BOARD
J. C. WILLEVER FIRST VICE-PRESIDENT

SYMBOLS
DL = Day Letter
NL = Night Letter
LC = Deferred Cable
NLT = Cable Night Letter
Ship Radiogram

The filing time shown in the date line on telegrams and day letters is STANDARD TIME at point of origin. Time of receipt is STANDARD TIME at point of destination

TO: ERIK VON STERNBERG, HOTEL SAVOY-PLAZA, NYC CONFIDENTIAL

MADAME X WARPATH STOP WHAT HAPPENED PREMIERE STOP

WHO GIRL NO TEST NO CONTRACT STOP DO NOT GET ON

TRAIN UNTIL EXPLAIN RL

WESTERN UNION 1201

CLASS OF SERVICE
This is a full-rate Telegram or Cablegram unless its deferred character is indicated by a suitable symbol above or preceding the address.

R. B. WHITE PRESIDENT
NEWCOMB CARLTON CHAIRMAN OF THE BOARD
J. C. WILLEVER FIRST VICE-PRESIDENT

SYMBOLS
DL = Day Letter
NL = Night Letter
LC = Deferred Cable
NLT = Cable Night Letter
Ship Radiogram

The filing time shown in the date line on telegrams and day letters is STANDARD TIME at point of origin. Time of receipt is STANDARD TIME at point of destination

TO: REUBEN LILIENTHAL, MONOLITHIC PICTURES

REGRET CALL UNSATISFACTORY STOP ANGEL

UNIQUE STOP MADAME X INSANE NOT I STOP

FOR ALL OUR SAKES DO NOT MISS SIGNING THIS GIRL EVS

WESTERN UNION 1201

CLASS OF SERVICE
This is a full-rate Telegram or Cablegram unless its deferred character is indicated by a suitable symbol above or preceding the address.

R. B. WHITE PRESIDENT
NEWCOMB CARLTON CHAIRMAN OF THE BOARD
J. C. WILLEVER FIRST VICE-PRESIDENT

SYMBOLS
DL = Day Letter
NL = Night Letter
LC = Deferred Cable
NLT = Cable Night Letter
Ship Radiogram

The filing time shown in the date line on telegrams and day letters is STANDARD TIME at point of origin. Time of receipt is STANDARD TIME at point of destination

TO: ERIK VON STERNBERG

NO TEST NO CONTRACT PERIOD RL

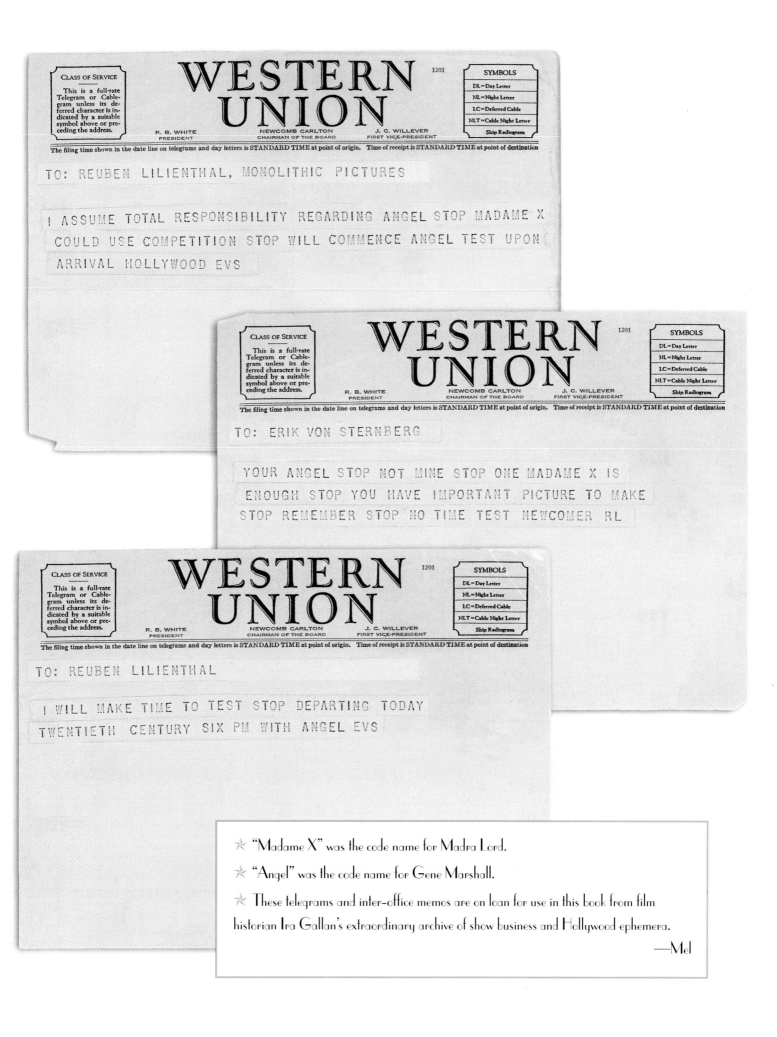

WESTERN UNION 1201

TO: REUBEN LILIENTHAL, MONOLITHIC PICTURES

I ASSUME TOTAL RESPONSIBILITY REGARDING ANGEL STOP MADAME X
COULD USE COMPETITION STOP WILL COMMENCE ANGEL TEST UPON
ARRIVAL HOLLYWOOD EVS

WESTERN UNION 1201

TO: ERIK VON STERNBERG

YOUR ANGEL STOP NOT MINE STOP ONE MADAME X IS
ENOUGH STOP YOU HAVE IMPORTANT PICTURE TO MAKE
STOP REMEMBER STOP NO TIME TEST NEWCOMER RL

WESTERN UNION 1201

TO: REUBEN LILIENTHAL

I WILL MAKE TIME TO TEST STOP DEPARTING TODAY
TWENTIETH CENTURY SIX PM WITH ANGEL EVS

✮ "Madame X" was the code name for Madra Lord.

✮ "Angel" was the code name for Gene Marshall.

✮ These telegrams and inter-office memos are on loan for use in this book from film historian Ira Gallan's extraordinary archive of show business and Hollywood ephemera.

—Mel

5

The Journey

CORA HARPER

From *Non-Stop Hollywood* syndicated column

Los Angeles Ledger

NON-STOP HOLLYWOOD

THE RAGE FOR GENE MARSHALL GROWS.

In all my years of stargazing, I have never witnessed such excitement generated by an unknown.

After photographs of Gene Marshall appeared in newspapers yesterday, my syndicate was flooded with calls pleading for details about the mysterious beauty discovered by Erik von Sternberg.

Practically a runaway debutante, Gene Marshall hails from Cos Cob, a smart village on the Connecticut–New York border, which she left half a year ago to seek her fortune in the big city. She is not quite eighteen.

Von Sternberg declares he will give Marshall a "suitable" role in "Blonde Lace," a romantic comedy he is lensing with Madra Lord and Trent Osborn. But there's trouble brewing in paradise, or at Monolithic, to be precise, as studio head Reuben Lilienthal is angered by the disruption of "Deep Devotion" and outraged that the director has hired a complete unknown without so much as a screen test.

A little green birdie tells me that a showdown is likely several days hence. Von Sternberg entrains tonight for Hollywood aboard the Twentieth Century to resume filming "Blonde Lace" later this week. With him is his lovely new protégée, accompanied by her mother. Also onboard will be Trent Osborn, Happy Trales, Ivy Jordan, and other Monolithic names.

Unless I miss my guess, an army of photographers will see them off at Grand Central.

They won't see Madra Lord, who changed her plans and took an airplane to the West Coast. Speaking of whom, let me add my opinion that it's a sign of true stardom when a celebrity graciously shares the limelight as Madra did with Gene Marshall the other evening. Imagine, Madra even posed for pictures with this obscure little usherette who might well become her competition in a few years. Talk about a lady who's each and every inch a star!

CONSTANCE BENNETT'S fling with Gilbert Roland appears to be all flung out after the lovebirds were spotted

IVY JORDAN

Erik always knew exactly how long to sustain a scene, on-screen or off. After fifteen minutes of pandemonium, he ended the photo session. I tagged along as Erik took Gene upstairs to the theater manager's office. My date somehow got lost—and the next time I hear from the poor Joe, it's 1944 and he's in the merchant marine! Trent vanished, too, chasing some quail, no doubt, while Madra grabbed Harry Hale and dragged him back to her hotel for a big fat earful.

Erik described *Blonde Lace* to Gene, saying he had a nice little part in it for her. But she must say yes or no right away to his proposition, as she had to go out on the train with the rest of us.

Gene said she better call her folks in Connecticut.

Once Gene convinced them that Erik meant business, her folks arrived in no time flat. By then, we had moved on to some nightclub after making a stop at the Savoy-Plaza, where I lent Gene one of my new Hattie Carnegies to wear.

ERIK VON STERNBERG

From *Eye for Beauty*

She was practically a child.

Gene's parents understandably were protective of their prize. I had to convince them that my intentions were honorable. It was a difficult proposition, as Dr. Marshall was unaware of my position in the cinema capital. "She may be your new discovery, but she is my daughter," he reminded me more than once. The idea of Gene journeying to a faraway sink-pit of sin and sensation did not sit well.

There we were, in the back room of the Stork Club, where the elder Marshalls looked conspicuously out of their New England element. I ordered a bottle of champagne for us—and a Coca-Cola for Gene, which suggested to her father that perhaps I had her best interests in mind.

"I am a father myself," I noted, telling them about Zena and our children. Her parents, I soon gathered, did not share Gene's enthusiasm for film. But both recognized the name of Zena Thor—how could they not?—and seemed reassured by my union with a legend such as she. "Oh, you're the one she gave up making movies for," said Mrs. Marshall, nodding.

I talked about the possibility of a seven-year contract for Gene that would gradually increase her salary if the studio exercised its options. I mentioned how Monolithic was one of Hollywood's top studios and how millions would jump for such a chance for their child. I said that Gene's role in *Blonde Lace* would be small but choice, and that she could probably return home in a few weeks. (For a short visit only, I secretly told myself.) All the while, I was as charming to them as I possibly knew how to be.

Dr. Marshall was impressed when Walter Winchell came over to our table. "Let me meet this new dream girl that everyone's talking about," said Walter. After a while, the earliest editions of the papers arrived with their coverage of the premiere. Mrs. Marshall was delighted by all the photos of Gene; Dr. Marshall looked resigned.

He turned to his daughter. "Do you want to go out there?" Gene said she really did. Dr. Marshall then informed me that Gene's mother would accompany her out to California.

"Agreed," I said eagerly, shaking his hand. "The studio will pay for everything."

"My goodness," cried Mrs. Marshall, "if Katie and I are going to Hollywood so soon, we have to get back to Cos Cob so I can pack my grip."

"In a moment," said Dr. Marshall, "right now, it's high time that Katie and I had a glass of champagne."

Harry Hale
From ASF's Oral History Project

After Erik's big surprise at the premiere, and the huge photo spreads in the papers next morning, I figured we'd have more than the usual press contingent at Grand Central Terminal. But nobody expected the extra swarm of movie fans. I assumed they were there for Madra and would be disappointed not to see her.

But no. They wanted to get a gander at Gene.

More than just movie fans, too. The Twentieth Century left at six, so it was the middle of rush hour in Grand Central when Gene arrived with her folks and Von Sternberg. All these commuters running for trains to Larchmont and Yonkers screeched to a halt just to watch her walk by. Even then Gene knew how to stop traffic.

There were so many people milling around, we finally had to get the station police to rope off the red carpet area leading to the train. Pictures, pictures, pictures.

I'll never forget Gene that day. She wore a snappy three-piece suit. It was, let me see, checked wool trimmed in fur, with a big brown hat and a muff to match. Red gloves. Cute.

IVY JORDAN

Transcontinental train travel was deluxe back then. Planes were still risky and no fun, besides, all cooped up in a crate for twenty or more hours and making a dozen landings for fuel.

But the trains were something else. Overnight to Chicago, then transfer the next morning to the Super Chief for two more days to Los Angeles. Terrific food, luxurious surroundings, beauty shop, masseuse, everything but a swimming pool. Interesting people aboard—Mrs. Roosevelt, Noël Coward, Lily Pons—and all the time in the world to spend with them. The Mono bunch had private drawing rooms. Gene and her mother shared the one originally reserved for Madra, who had flown home in a snit. Probably on her own broomstick.

Saying good-bye to Dr. Marshall at Grand Central was hard for Gene. "If I can't go with you and your mother, here's someone else who can," he said, handing her an old teddy bear. Then the tears started.

Actually, somebody else did go with them. At the train, Dr. Marshall ran into an old chum who'd been his roomie at Harvard. Edward Ames, an attorney, a distinguished-looking old coot now living in Pasadena. Evidently rich as Croesus. Heading home after a business trip east and only too glad to keep an eye on Gene and her mother.

TRENT OSBORN
From *My Bed of Roses*

That ride back was mostly a blur for me. Nothing to do and everything to drink. I got involved in a poker game. Wound up losing ten thousand dollars between New York and Chicago. Then I met a redhead who said she liked me better than Tyrone Power. She saw me through Chicago and then some. Considering what she wound up costing me, I should have stayed in the poker game.

ERIK VON STERNBERG
From *Eye for Beauty*

It was essential for Gene to look a vision of loveliness.

She wore a simple winter ensemble when we left New York, but it was scarcely a thing for stepping off the train in California. Judging by the crowd seeing her off, I felt that many others would be craving a glimpse along the way, so it was essential that Gene look divine.

As soon as the train departed, I joined Gene and her mother to see what she had packed. Of course she had nothing suitable. So I decided to spend our brief time in Chicago shopping. It was hardly Paris, but I anticipated we could pick up a few decent things.

Mrs. Marshall said no, that they didn't bring money to buy the sort of ensembles I proposed. I assured her money was no object. I would be happy to advance any necessary amount. Gene looked pleased, though her mother seemed doubtful. "A man buying Katie clothes? Won't people talk?"

"They will say even worse things if she arrives in Hollywood looking like a little mouse," I told her.

Gene Marshall

Harry Hale
From ASF's Oral History Project

Having Cora Harper aboard with us did not make my job easier. Although taken with Gene, and feeling a proprietary interest in the girl's discovery, Cora was a professional snoop. One of the biggest in the gossip business—if not always the sharpest.

Lucky for me, Cora's daily newspaper column kept her busy, sifting through telegrams from spies and banging on her typewriter in her compartment. Funny—Trent was on one of his periodic benders right there on the same train, but old Cora never got wind of it.

Cora was scheduled to make one of her radio broadcasts while overnight in Chicago. She insisted that Gene appear. So I made a deal—if Gene did her program, Cora had to leave her alone for the rest of the trip. That was all right by Cora, as long as the radio thing happened.

Erik was none too thrilled with my bargain, but understood its necessity. He began obsessing over Gene's appearance on the broadcast. "She's still an ordinary girl," he kept saying, "but for her radio debut, she needs to be extraordinary!"

Ivy Jordan

After dinner, we went to the club car to relax. It was like being in a little art deco nightclub going seventy miles an hour. Mostly the Mono gang was there, listening to the piano player, a good one who knew every song in the book. Happy Trales, who'd been dipping in the moonshine, favored us with every single verse of "The Last Round-Up."

Having had a couple of Rob Roys myself, I launched into "Bye, Bye, Blackbird." Now, I have what is known as a small but disagreeable voice, so when I paused for breath, the pianist quickly switched to an old Irving Berlin tune.

Gene said she loved that song.

Erik wondered whether she could sing it for him.

"Of course she can," piped up Mrs. Marshall. "Katie is very musical. She got that from my side of the family. Go ahead and show them, honey."

Well, maybe she would, if the pianist had the sheet music there.

He did. So Gene went over to the piano and sang "Blue Skies." Turns out she had a lovely voice. Soft and a bit husky, like peach velvet.

56

Gee, I thought, the kid can sing. Before you know it, Erik will put her in a musical. But he was way ahead of me.

"What would you think about doing that song on Cora Harper's radio program tomorrow night?" he asked Gene.

She thought that singing would be easier than coming up with clever things to say.

Two minutes later, Erik had hustled everybody out of the club car and was hunkering down with Gene and the piano player to rehearse.

HARRY HALE
From ASF's Oral History Project

It was long past midnight when the Twentieth Century rolled through Buffalo. Gene, poor kid, was pooped from the excitement and had gone to bed maybe an hour before. Her mother was this fresh-air fiend and had cracked open the window in their compartment—and left the shade up, too.

Now I don't know what happened. The Twentieth Century was an express. It wasn't supposed to stop. But somehow the train slowed down enough so some eager-beaver news photographer waiting in the railroad yard was able to grab a picture of Gene through the compartment window.

His flashbulb wakes both Gene and Mrs. Marshall—the old lady was the one who screamed—but by the time they rush into the corridor to tell the conductor what's going on, the photographer is half a mile down the track, heading for his newspaper.

Anyway, it turned out to be one hell of a photo. I couldn't have planned it better myself. Nothing revealing, you know, just this sweet picture of Gene, all tuckered out and all tucked in, dreaming away in her berth.

The photo hit the wire services, and by the time the Twentieth Century reached Chicago, that beddy-bye picture was in all the papers coast to coast. SLEEPING BEAUTY, read the headline for most of them.

GENE MARSHALL, Hollywood's newest princess, dreams of a bright future.

You couldn't pay for publicity like that.

CORA HARPER
From *Non-Stop Hollywood* syndicated column

Los Angeles Ledger

NON-STOP HOLLYWOOD

ERIK VON STERNBERG AND HIS NEW FIND GENE MARSHALL blew into the Windy City this morning like a hurricane. Refusing all interviews, they rushed off to the Sherman House and thence to several exclusive shops. A vast amount of Monolithic money was spent equipping Miss Marshall for the rigors of her journey west.

Which is intriguing, since a little green birdie advises me that the lovely Miss M has yet to sign a contract.

Not at all studio procedure, but one expects that Von Sternberg knows what he's about. Beautiful girls must have beautiful things.

I expect we will see something spectacular on Miss Marshall's back when she appears on my broadcast tonight at 9 P.M. over the Blue Network.

IT'S DEFINITE! MGM will star Garbo as uranium-discovering French scientist

IVY JORDAN

Mom Marshall said she couldn't bear to see Erik buy up a lot of clothes they couldn't possibly afford and asked me to chaperone the shopping expedition.

People who think that Erik was dictatorial on the set never saw him charge into a department store. Sales clerks to the right of him, managers to the left of him, all soon reduced to jelly. Nothing was good enough for Erik's new star.

I felt like Cinderella's pumpkin, watching him dress up Gene. Hats, shoes, gloves, stockings. He was about to storm the lingerie department when Gene told him she'd rather choose those things herself. That was fine by Erik—he was having too much fun giving breakdowns to the floor walkers. "Hideous," he'd scream at some lovely outfit. "Awful! Do you only dress the wives of butchers?"

After raiding half a dozen stores, Erik was able to dig up enough glad rags to get Gene to Hollywood. Then came fittings. Since the shops were closing, Erik simply kidnapped a couple of seamstresses and took them back to the hotel. Mom Marshall moaned and asked for a Bromo after she saw the bellboys come staggering in with mountains of boxes.

As the fitters worked, Erik gave Gene one of those squinty-eyed stares that meant something was cooking inside that brain of his. Finally, he announced, "I believe we'll change the color of your hair."

Gene stared back and wondered whether it made a difference on the radio. Erik looked at his watch, screamed something in German, and rushed her away, leaving Mrs. Marshall to worry about getting the dresses finished.

ANONYMOUS
From *The Chicago Tribune,* "Tune-Up Time" radio column

Gene Marshall, Hollywood's newest sensation—only she hasn't even arrived in Hollywood yet—made a surprise appearance on Cora Harper's "Non-Stop Hollywood" program last night, broadcast from the Sherman House ballroom. And boy, what a surprise it was.

After typical gushings by the pink-haired gossip columnist, who shamelessly credits herself with making Marshall such a hot item with the public, the young lady was trotted before the microphone to sing.

Backed by Leon Coleman's Windy City Eight, Marshall warbled "Blue Skies." She handled the ballad in a graceful fashion, interpreting the words with warmth while singing in an angelic whisper. She's as sweet to the ear as she's easy on the eye.

For a supposed novice, Marshall shows a lot of professionalism and demonstrates an intimate way with the mike that could land her steady employment on the airwaves anytime she wants. When she finished, the audience whistled and stamped its approval.

If Marshall's new bosses are smart, they'll put her to work in musicals.

Trent Osborn

From *My Bed of Roses*

In the morning, Harry paid for the damage to my hotel suite and put me and Gene in the same taxi. Her mother crammed in with us, too. Maybe she was nervous I'd make a pass at her baby. But I was too hung over even to dream of such things.

Gene had her nose pressed to the glass, as she'd never seen Chicago. When we arrived at the station, a dozen flashbulbs went off, and Gene jerked her head back so fast that her hat nearly flew off. The instant we were out of the car, a bunch of fans swarmed.

"Can I have your autograph, Miss Marshall?" they started asking, shoving their books in her surprised face.

Gene insisted she hadn't done anything yet.

"We heard you sing on the radio last night. You're wonderful!"

Gene looked doubtful, but she signed anyway. The way I felt, I was having trouble signing my name at all, but luckily the fans seemed more interested in Gene than me. But with the crush of people and all the flashbulbs exploding, I felt myself going green. Gene saw what was happening and somehow managed to yank me through the mob and safely onto the train before my churning stomach let go.

6

Meanwhile . . . Back in Hollywood

CORA HARPER

From *Non-Stop Hollywood* syndicated column

Los Angeles Ledger

NON-STOP HOLLYWOOD

 ANN SHERIDAN may be the Oomph Girl, but a little green birdie tells me that the biggest noise in Hollywood can be overheard at Monolithic, where the studio is dusting off the welcome mat for newcomer Gene Marshall....

CUTEST NEW TWOSOME in town is those teenaged thespians Jackie Cooper and Bonita Granville who met over ice-cream sodas at Schwab's and quickly fell

From *Maharajah of the Movies*

Madra Lord screamed her way through three secretaries and a bodyguard into the mogul's office. "It's not enough that your lousy Kraut sabotaged my opening," she shrilled at Lilienthal. "Now he thinks he can shove that little nobody into my new picture!"

"Simmer down, Madra," said Lilienthal, retreating behind his desk. "Whatever fool thing that Erik did the other night grabbed us a lot of headlines, and we're doing good business."

Critics had screened *Deep Devotion* days before the aborted premiere, and reviews were favorable, especially for Lord's portrayal of a reformed jewel thief. The initial box-office response was promising.

"I don't care!" snapped the irate star. "I don't want that Marshall girl anywhere near *Blonde Lace*!"

"Nothing is set in stone," Lilienthal soothed her. "She may be coming out here with Erik, but she has no contract. She hasn't even been tested. I don't sign anyone to do anything here without a test."

"Yeah, well, you better not be testing her!"

"It's a tiny role," he reminded Lord. "A walk-on in a nightclub scene."

"I'm telling you, Rubi, if that girl walks on—I'm walking off!"

Lilienthal's face flushed maroon beneath its deep tan. "Listen to me, Miss Mabel Lorkovic. I run this operation, not you."

Lord rose grandly above Lilienthal's reference to her humble Milwaukee beginnings. "From what I hear, this joint is being run right into the mud," she retorted.

The studio boss turned his back, surveying the Monolithic lot through the wide windows beyond his desk. "Nothing's wrong that a few big hits won't cure," he declared.

"I'm the one who gives you your hits! Not that phony baloney with the monocle," she shrilled. "You should take better care of me instead of coddling Erik's crazy whims, or just maybe I'll suddenly get too sick to finish *Blonde Lace*."

Lilienthal whirled around, snarling. "I'll give you sick! Don't ever threaten me like that, Miss Lord. Pull a fake illness on me in the middle of a picture and your contract gets canceled."

"What fake illness? Who's to say whether I'm sick or not? You couldn't prove a thing." A nasty smile flashed across Lord's face as she raised an elegantly gloved hand to her throat. "Why, Rubi dear, I do believe that I've got a cold coming on. Oh, that darned New York weather. I certainly hope it doesn't turn into something worse," she mocked him. "So—how do you like them apples, big boy?"

Now it was Lilienthal's turn to smile. He pressed a button on his desk. His secretary's head popped in.

"Did you get all that down, Miss Hardy?"

"Yes, sir," the secretary said, reading aloud from her stenography pad. "I certainly hope it doesn't turn into something worse. So, how do you like them apples—"

"Look at that—I must have left the intercom switch on," the studio chief chuckled. "Miss Hardy never knows when to stop taking dictation."

"You snake. You louse. You son of—"

"Careful, Madra, Miss Hardy's vocabulary isn't as extensive as yours."

Miss Hardy, in the outer office, heard a screeching electronic noise just as the intercom went dead. Then glass crashed behind the closed door. Madra Lord appeared a moment later and stalked past the silent staff. A buzzer sounded on the secretary's console.

"Yes, sir?"

"Call the glaziers," said Lilienthal. "And get me a new intercom, will you?"

BENNY MAJORS
Madra Lord's former agent

Madra was riding pretty high about that time. She was up for an Academy Award that year for *He Married His Boss.* Ever see it? Snappy picture. Madra plays this cosmetics tycoon and Fred MacMurray takes a job as her personal secretary.

Now Madra never had what you'd call a sense of humor, but with the right director and material, she could be awfully funny when she wanted.

On-screen, I mean. Off camera was something else. Boy, don't I know it!

Madra was up against stiff competition—let's see—Bette Davis and Katharine Hepburn were among the nominees, if I remember rightly. But being so comical in *He Married His Boss* represented a big change of pace for Madra, whose specialty was ladies' sudsers. The handicappers thought she stood a fair chance of grabbing the Oscar. And, oh, boy, she wanted it real bad.

Madra wasn't at all pleased about the progress on *Blonde Lace.* That picture was trouble from the start. The script was lousy and Von Sternberg was being a crazy man on the set.

64

Madra Lord

So Gene Marshall's dawning at the *Deep Devotion* premiere was the poison cherry on Madra's parfait, if you know what I mean.

GEORGIA JAMES
Screenwriter
From Naomi Roth's *Hollywood Talks: The Myths and Their Making*
(New York: Brinton Brothers Publishing, 1977)

Sure, I know everyone considers *Blonde Lace* a classic. But it was a pain in my sweet cheeks from the giddyap.

Erik first saw it as a romantic escapade. A small-town detective on vacation hits a swank nightclub in the big city. He meets a red-hot widow whose husband willed her the joint just before he cools. So this dick and this chick click together just as a gambling racket tries to muscle in on her club. The running gag was that as heroic as the detective tries to be, the dame is the one always pulling him out of the soup.

There was talk about getting Joan Bennett or maybe Hedy Lamarr for the part, but Madra grabbed it. I forget how we named it.

Well, God knows major movies have been made from worse scenarios, but *Blonde Lace* refused to behave. Normally, it'd be shelved, but Erik had already snowed Lilienthal into giving a green light before we had it written.

So the sets were built. This nightclub setting with stairs going up to Jesus and huge mirrors. The widow's penthouse. Several other ritzy locations.

We started shooting even as I was rewriting. Erik knew it was a piece of limburger, but believed we'd squeak through on style. Too bad that Erik couldn't seem to hoo-doo his usual magic on the set. Production bogged down, and pretty soon Lilienthal got wind there was trouble on the farm.

The boss told us we better have this script licked by the time everyone came back from the *Deep Devotion* premiere. Or else. So after powwowing with Erik, I knocked out a rewrite over a long and thirsty weekend in Palm Springs. The new script was an improvement, but only like a broken arm is better than a broken back.

One of the things we worked out before he left town was a bit part for a beauty who'd play a little flower girl in the club. Madra's character, Vera, was going to fire this girl just to establish how she was tougher than she looked. That was the role Erik intended to give Gene Marshall when he discovered her.

From the Original Screenplay of *Blonde Lace*

<u>BLONDE LACE / DRAFT 7</u>

                    VERA
    Well, aren't you a pretty little thing! You're new here,
aren't you?

                  MARJORIE
    Yes. Mr. Ellerbe hired me last week.

                    VERA
    So I thought. I happen to be Mrs. Ellerbe.

                  MARJORIE
    Oh. I'm so sorry about your loss. (Hands Vera a flower.)
Mr. Ellerbe was kind to me.

                    VERA
    I'm sure he was. But you better save being so sorry for
yourself.

                  MARJORIE
    Why, Mrs. Ellerbe?

                    VERA
    Don't you get it? My late husband is gone. But I'm here
to say that you're through.

                  MARJORIE
    What?

                    VERA
    You little nobody. Don't play so innocent. I don't need
you around here to remind me of my late husband's taste in
young women.

                  MARJORIE
    But ...
                    VERA
    Raoul will pay you off. Get back to finishing school, kid.
You're already finished here.

Hell, it wasn't much of a part. She just had to look cute in a short skirt. I figured any of our contract cupcakes around the lot would do. There's no shortage of pretty in Hollywood.

So I was startled when all this big back-and-forth began between Erik and Lilienthal over bringing a girl from New York to play Marjorie. Then Erik wired me from Chicago about fluffing up Marjorie's role.

Now, if it had been some other director, I would guess that he was sleeping with the girl. Standard Hollywood practice, don't you know? I've seen all too many directors go down in flames over a skirt.

But Erik didn't work that way. He only made love through his camera lens. That's why I knew that this new girl must be the real deal.

When that "Sleeping Beauty" photo appeared in the *Los Angeles Times,* I got my first tip-off on what Erik was all excited about. So that morning, I started working on a snappy scene in the checkroom between Marjorie and Jane—that's the role Ivy Jordan was playing, a smart-mouthed hatcheck girl.

When I came back from lunch, I had a message that the boss wanted me pronto. Seeing Reuben Lilienthal was like going to the principal's office. Only worse. He had this gigantic spread on the top floor of the administration building, with about fifty miles of carpet to cross before you reached his desk, which was this huge mahogany thing raised like a throne. The joke was that Lilienthal really believed he was Napoleon in a former life. Well, come to think of it, he was short enough.

Quite a layout. Behind his desk was a wall of windows, with an incredible view overlooking the studio.

Only this time when I went in to see Lilienthal, one of the windows was being replaced. He ordered the hired hands out and said to me, "You're not to fiddle with *Blonde Lace* any more. Consider the script frozen."

I tried to play dumb, but he wasn't having it.

"Don't tell me. Do you think I don't know everything that goes on around here?"

I said it was just one tiny little scene, but he refused to listen.

"The script stays as it is until Erik gets here. That's final. Get me?"

"But what about this new girl he found?"

"Never mind about her."

"Well, you're the boss."

"Maybe you'll kindly remind your pal Von Sternberg when you talk to him next."

He pointed to the door. I hightailed it out of there as fast as I could.

7

The Journey Continues

CORA HARPER

From *Non-Stop Hollywood* syndicated column

𝕷𝖔𝖘 𝕬𝖓𝖌𝖊𝖑𝖊𝖘 𝕷𝖊𝖉𝖌𝖊𝖗

NON-STOP HOLLYWOOD

THE KANSAS PLAINS RUSH BY as I pen today's column from my private compartment aboard the glamorous Super Chief. Somewhere in the next car, Erik von Sternberg is coaching Gene Marshall in the role she will play in "Blonde Lace," a picture far from completion. But evidently it's one that many people already want to see, judging by the hordes swarming the La Salle Street Station hungry to get a glimpse of the lissome newcomer.

Listeners who heard my radio program from Chicago already demand that Gene should sing a number in "Blonde Lace." Look out, Betty Grable—that's all I can say.

JOAN CRAWFORD CONFIDES that she is so thrilled by adoptive motherhood that she plans to get lucky Christina another brother or sister as soon as she completes

ERIK VON STERNBERG

From *Eye for Beauty*

Gene was much more a junior miss than a Hollywood myth on that westward journey.

The legend goes that I transformed Gene à la Pygmalion during those two days between Chicago and California. It is a flattering story, but one not altogether accurate. Gene essentially had everything to begin with. I simply focused and refined certain aspects.

And that process took longer than our trip together. After all, there is just so much one can do in a railway car.

But I knew Gene had to appear as stunning as she could be on the day she arrived in Hollywood. My telegrams and long-distance conversations with Reuben Lilienthal had not gone favorably. The studio head resisted my pleas for a long-term contract for Gene. He even refused to grant her a role in *Blonde Lace*. It was crucial that Reuben's first glimpse of Gene should dazzle him.

I summoned the train's beautician and we set to work lightening Gene's honey-blonde hair. As Missouri and Kansas rolled by, we juggled with basins, towels, and tints. Too platinum. Too lemony. Too straw-colored. Gene uncomplainingly endured our ministrations until Ivy strolled in and remarked, "I hope you've got Gene a cute little turban somewhere in those hat boxes. Because if you dye her hair one more time today, she's going to be bald."

We desisted. By now, Gene's hair was a mass of champagne curls that heightened the intensity of her eyes. The look might not have been perfect, but it would do nicely for her Hollywood arrival. Especially in a dramatic French-blue ensemble I had carefully chosen in Chicago. Blue was Reuben's favorite color.

As her hair dried, I took the opportunity to coach Gene on her deportment. There was a coltish way about her that would not further the soignée image that I had conceived. We worked together for hours on simple things like walking, sitting, and gracefully moving across a room. With Mrs. Marshall stationed at one end of a corridor and I at the other, I made Gene walk back and forth along the car one afternoon. Eventually Gene was gliding about like a swan.

Harry Hale
From ASF's Oral History Project

She really was a phenomenon. I wish I could say Gene's sensational dawning was due to my expertise, but it was something out of my control.

By the time we left Chicago, I realized that Gene was big news. The public's awareness of her was snowballing like nothing I'd ever seen before. The uproar at the premiere, the "Sleeping Beauty" picture, the radio broadcast, the mobs of people in Chicago, the glowing reports about her in Winchell's, Harper's, Parson's, and all the other columns had ignited national interest.

Telegrams poured in from newspapers and magazines wanting interviews. Erik dismissed them. "No interviews until we arrive in Hollywood." He allowed pictures, thank God. At our stops in Kansas City and Albuquerque, I trotted Gene out onto the Super Chief's observation platform to smile and wave, and smile and wave again.

She was a natural. When I told her so, Gene giggled that she was just pretending to be a movie star. We had a good laugh together over that.

DR. ARTHUR D. HUFF

From *20th Century: The War Years, 1939–45* (New York: Advanced Publications, 1999)

Chapter Eight: Stormy Weather

February 1941 was a particularly gray month of dismal winter weather across America. Reports of labor strikes and crop losses intensified the bleak war news from abroad. With all Europe ablaze and the Pacific scene growing increasingly dark, the American home front was jumping with nervous gaiety.

One of the era's most remarkable stories detailed the instant movie stardom of Gene Marshall. A beautiful girl who had never stepped upon a stage or before a camera, the seventeen-year-old Marshall was whisked off to Hollywood by a director who met her at a New York film premiere. Breathless accounts of Marshall's discovery proved a perfect antidote to the news from abroad for anxious Americans hungry for some brightness in their lives.

As the train taking Marshall to Hollywood sped west, newspaper photographs of the blonde, blue-eyed girl—a classic American beauty—ignited a blaze of interest that swept across the country like a prairie fire. Reporters and columnists tumbled over each other to tell readers anything they could learn or manufacture about the newcomer. Radio broadcasts speculated on her future. Pundits wondered whether Marshall could possibly live up to her publicity. Comedians cracked jokes. At stops along the route, Marshall was greeted by increasing crowds eager to see this modern-day Cinderella on her way to the ball.

Because Marshall was cocooned aboard a train and unavailable to the press, a Garbo-esque allure was soon attached to her. In less than a week, Marshall shot from complete anonymity to being practically a household name.

IVY JORDAN

Harry declared that the demand for Gene was greater than anything he'd ever known. But it wasn't until we hit the Far West that I understood how deeply she had registered around the country.

It was early morning when we rolled into Williams, Arizona. Ever been there? Aside from the Grand Canyon, there's not much to see. Talk about the middle of nowhere at 3 A.M.

Loud voices in the corridor. I stuck my head out. Erik and Harry were huddled with the chief conductor, talking urgently with Mom Marshall.

"But she's asleep, Mr. Von Sternberg, and you said yourself that Katie needed rest."

Looking worried, Erik said they had no choice but to wake her.

The conductor said that an enormous crowd of people had gathered on the tracks and wouldn't budge until they got a look at Gene. They'd been waiting for hours.

Gene appeared, rubbing sleep from her eyes, wondering what was wrong.

"It appears you've got a local fan club," Harry told her. "You need to make a quick personal appearance."

We all looked outside and, sure enough, the platform was packed. You wouldn't believe it. The whole thing looked like Central Casting for a John Ford movie. Cowboys, Indians, little kids, old ladies right off a covered wagon, everybody for miles around, it seemed.

Mrs. Marshall said she'd try to get Gene ready quickly. But the conductor declared the train was already behind schedule. Couldn't Miss Marshall say hello to them in her bathrobe?

"She certainly will not," Erik declared. "It's snowing out there."

After Gene said she'd talk to the crowd regardless of the weather, Erik darted back with his own overcoat and threw it around her.

It was a military greatcoat in camel's hair, with a huge fur collar, much too big for Gene. Erik made a rapid adjustment, however, and it suddenly seemed to fit. Then we silently marched down the corridor like a royal party going to a firing squad.

The conductor opened the door and let down the steps. Then I saw it happen. That magical thing that Gene

could do. One moment, she was an apprehensive teen in slippers and a man's over-coat. The next she was a goddess. Her chin went up, her blue eyes blazed, and a radiant smile lit her face. She stepped away from her mother and Erik and out into the doorway.

ERIK VON STERNBERG

From *Eye for Beauty*

Gene scarcely said a thing, but they nearly swooned with delight at the sight of her.

A newfound princess welcomed by her people, that's what she was.

The amazing incident in Arizona convinced me beyond all doubt that if Gene's magic could be transferred to film, she might become one of its supreme artists. If—that was the crucial point. I had no idea whether her beauty and appeal would register on celluloid. The camera is an unpredictable lover.

For that matter, I had no idea whether I'd even have the opportunity to film Gene. I had alienated Monolithic's most influential star and infuriated its owner. Gene had signed no contract, as none had been offered by the studio, and her new adviser, Edward Ames, was counseling her to consider other possibilities.

He was frank about it. "We have some intriguing opportunities," the old man said, displaying a yellow sheaf of telegrams. "Paramount. MGM. Twentieth Century-Fox. They appear highly eager to engage Miss Marshall."

"They're offering Gene contracts?"

"Yes, indeed, depending upon how her screen tests turn out. Quite attractive deals, too. And not only movies. That Chicago broadcast has enthused radio and recording people no little."

"Her gifts would be wasted on radio."

"That is as may be," Ames replied, "but I don't observe Monolithic approaching Miss Marshall to make any pictures."

"I'll be more than happy to put Gene under my personal contract."

"That's kind of you, sir, but I doubt whether you have the resources to do it," he said, eyeing me coolly. "Perhaps you could prior to all this publicity, but no longer. Alfred Marshall would never forgive me if I allowed his only child to accept a substandard agreement."

My face must have fallen through the dining car floor. "Look," said Ames, softening. "I can understand that Monolithic might not want to commit to an entirely untested commodity. So test away with her, and if the studio is pleased, we'll negotiate."

"I can't thank you enough."

"Of course," Ames continued, "should Monolithic delay unduly, I have no alternative but to discuss Miss Marshall's future with others. In the meantime, I expect you or your studio to continue to cover her complete expenses."

"That will all be arranged," I assured him. "I've already wired ahead to the Beverly Fairmont Hotel."

"Fine," said Ames, shaking my hand. "I'll put these other offers away for now."

It was a close call. But I was not confident regarding the studio's intentions. Ominous silence had greeted my last telegrams. However, my immediate concern was getting Gene ready for arrival later that morning. No doubt the press corps and fans would be waiting in droves at the station, as well as Lilienthal and his executives. Monolithic always welcomed their stars with considerable fanfare, and although Gene was yet to be a star, the national uproar over my discovery guaranteed a major reception.

TRENT OSBORN

From My Bed of Roses

My valet managed to throw me into a cold shower when we were still an hour outside of Pasadena. Nobody in the industry took the train into Los Angeles. Pasadena was closer to Beverly Hills, and that's where the studios always greeted arriving stars. Figuring that Monolithic would throw out the welcome mat in a big way for us, I made a special effort to look spiffy.

I wasn't the only one. Erik was charging up and down the corridor, snapping orders. He sent Ivy back to her room twice to change outfits. Happy Trales was clanking around in his silver spurs and white ten-gallon hat. Gene looked perfectly lovely in a blue suit precisely tailored to show off her charms. "You're blonder than I remembered," I joked.

A hard rain was pelting the windows as the train rolled into the station. "Beware of this California sunshine," I told Gene. "Not everything's as bright as it seems."

IVY JORDAN

I knew we were in trouble when I stepped off the train. Hollywood is a company town, and I guess people had their backs up over all the publicity Gene received. Raising the flag for an established star is standard, but making a fuss over an unknown celebrity is something else again. It's one thing to make headlines and it's another to make movies.

There was a satisfying number of people at the station—real people, you understand—to cheer Gene's arrival. But only the barest minimum of Monolithic brass was there on the platform. One of the Mono vice presidents presented Gene with a bouquet—nobody gave me anything—and then we posed for pictures. Ten seconds, tops, and then the executives scrammed like we had smallpox. Not a favorable sign. Newspapers had sent photographers, but I couldn't find the cameramen from Mono's newsreel division, which usually recorded our official comings and goings. That was a bad omen, too.

Opposite Page: Trent Osborn

Worse than anything, there wasn't a sign of Rubi Lilienthal.

Erik's face paled when informed that the big boss wasn't going to show. An important budget meeting, they said. Harry Hale looked downright sick over the news. "I guess the boss must be digging in his heels," he whispered, shaking his head.

Gene was disappointed not to be meeting Rubi, but she and her mother were soon busy saying good-bye to old man Ames. His son was there to meet him, a yummy college boy named Paul. A 14-karat dreamboat, believe me. I gave Paul my brightest smile, but he was already offering to show Gene the local sights whenever she wanted. She beamed at him gratefully.

"I am afraid Miss Marshall will be far too occupied for now to accept your invitation," snooted Erik.

Too bad, I thought. A date with a nice-looking fellow like young Master Ames might be just the thing to cheer a girl after a long trip.

The photographers were gone by then, and the fans were rapidly melting away. As the Ameses left, Paul kept turning around for one more glimpse of Gene. Did I mention the rain? It was hammering on the roof as Erik walked us out of the station to the studio car sent for the Marshalls.

But instead of the usual mile-long Monolithic limousine, a station wagon waited. A nice Ford, with the studio's crest painted on its wooden paneling, but still a station wagon. Gene might as well be a piece of furniture. Erik swore something in German.

"Idiots!" he spat, then spun on his heel and marched off into the downpour, leaving us flat.

Gene and her mother looked uncertain. "I could kill for a cup of coffee," I said, rapping on the windshield to wake up the driver. "Let's go over to my house."

8

Hello Hollywood!

CORA HARPER,

From *Non-Stop Hollywood* syndicated column

Los Angeles Ledger

NON-STOP HOLLYWOOD

THE FILM COLONY IS ABUZZ over the shabby way Monolithic treated its new find, Gene Marshall, on her very first day in California.

Instead of welcoming Gene with open arms, the studio all but ignored her at the station. Photos were taken, a few words of greeting were muttered, and then everyone simply vanished.

The very heavens wept at the sight of this forlorn beauty and her darling mother standing forgotten amid their luggage in Pasadena, utterly deserted by Erik von Sternberg and the heartless Monolithic crew.

It's unbelievable to me that a studio could be so cavalier about a lass who has garnered them such national attention. I am receiving bags of mail from radio-land listeners who thrilled to hear Gene make her singing debut on my broadcast earlier this week.

Fortunately, good gal Ivy Jordan personally drove the Marshalls to their hotel. If mother and daughter have any idea of how poorly they've been treated, they'll be packing for the next train east. However, one studio's bad meet may be another one's passion. Reps from rival companies are said to be contacting Gene with an eye toward signing her. It serves Reuben Lilienthal right if this wonder girl gets snatched out from under him.

MEANWHILE, OVER AT WARNER BROS., Humphrey Bogart is being threatened with suspension for refusing to play another outlaw in "Bad Men of Missouri,"

BENNY MAJORS

Look, just because I was Madra's agent doesn't mean I did all her dirty work. She was capable of making mischief on her own, thank you. So while Gene Marshall was still on the train, Madra was dialing everybody she knew to dish up a lot of lies. I can't recall any details after all these years, but I bet whatever terrible things Madra could dream up, she spewed out.

Anyway, the feeling back then was that all the publicity Gene had received was a crazy kind of fluke that would be forgotten overnight. Hollywood had seen plenty of those nine-day wonders before.

Don't forget, millions of discoveries before Gene had been publicized to the skies and never heard from again. Anna Sten, for instance, who Sam Goldwyn swore was going to be the new Garbo.

Anyway, Von Sternberg made a mistake by announcing that Gene was going to be Monolithic's great new star without so much as making a long-distance call to clear it with Lilienthal. You didn't do things like that back then. That's why Gene got the official cold shoulder. Nobody was going to tell Lilienthal who he was supposed to treat like a star.

Madra was pretty pleased by the way it all turned out. "So much for little Miss Nobody," she said.

ALICE MARSHALL
To Dr. Alfred Marshall

Dear Allie:

Well, we're here. The hotel has put us in this cute little two-bedroom bungalow in a garden behind the main building. There's a lovely pool and even a croquet field on the grounds.

You have seen the newspapers, so you know that Katie has made a big success on the way out. But now there is some hitch at the studio. The people seem pleasant, but nobody said anything about Katie's screen test. Maybe that's just how they do things, but from the way Mr. VS had been talking, I assumed they were going to rush her in front of the camera right away.

Katie seems a little disappointed, but she's not letting on. I was going to ask Katie if she wanted to add a line, but she's not here right now. Maybe she went to look at the croquet field. It was raining this morning, but the weather has cleared nicely. Since I have a lot of things to unpack, I am going to close now. I miss you, Dear, and will write again soon.

Much love, Allie

P.S. I hope you're remembering to take your fruit salts.

ERIK VON STERNBERG
From *Eye for Beauty*

I was beside myself with chagrin.

After dropping my bags at home, I rushed to Monolithic and went directly to Reuben's luxuriously gloomy lair. I marched up to Miss Hardy, his loyal protector, who hovered before the massive doors to the producer's chambers. "I demand to see him instantly!"

"He's been in there with the bankers all morning," said Miss Hardy.

Just then, the doors opened and several businessmen walked out with Reuben. He looked at me coldly and made introductions. I hid my rage beneath my best continental manners.

"I understand you've found the studio a new star," said one of the gentlemen politely.

"She's a real pip!" said another, jovially patting my arm.

"We are going to discuss Miss Marshall's future right now," I smiled.

As Miss Hardy escorted the bankers out, Reuben strode back to his desk. I followed, voicing dismay at his attitude toward my discovery. "I don't rush to the station to meet every little girl who's brought here to test," he replied. "I have other responsibilities around here."

"I've brought you a treasure!"

"That's what you say."

"Even those bourgeois money men knew who she was!"

"I'm impressed—that's an amazing publicity stunt you've pulled off," shrugged Reuben. "Harry gets a big fat bonus. But we could've just as easily had a fiasco, thanks to your little drama in the aisles. Tell me, Erik, did you plant the girl there? Where did you really meet her?"

"Gene truly was working as an usherette at the Regency that night. I swear to it."

"Yeah? I've heard some stories about her," he said, wrinkling his nose.

"Who knows Gene here in California?" Then the source struck me. "Madra!"

"Never mind that. You're behind schedule on *Blonde Lace*. I've given the go-ahead to Georgia's latest draft and you start shooting again tomorrow."

"But first I must make Gene's tests."

"I have half a mind to send that damned girl of yours back home on the next train," said Reuben darkly. "But then we'd be a national laughingstock if I did that, wouldn't we?"

It was then that I heard a familiar voice ask if she could come in. We both turned. There in the doorway stood Gene.

GEORGIA JAMES

From *Hollywood Talks*

Jiminy Christmas, I haven't a clue how Gene materialized inside the studio. Guess the guards at the front gate fell for her. Or maybe they knew her from the papers. Anyway, I saw this gorgeous youngster strolling across the lot. It took me a few seconds to match the real deal with all the photos I'd seen.

But looking at Gene in the flesh, I thought, oh boy, the camera will dish her up with a spoon.

She was new out here, Gene said, and needed to find Mr. Lilienthal's office. I introduced myself and offered to show the way.

For all of her looks, Gene seemed like a nice little thing, a sweet, unassertive teenager. But when we arrived at Lilienthal's suite, I noticed a curious thing happen.

As we entered, it was suddenly as if Gene became—I don't know how to describe this—bigger somehow. Luminous.

Tough little Miss Hardy, who'd seen every top dog in Hollywood scratch at Lilienthal's door down through the years, got one glimpse of Gene and lickety-split ushered her right into his inner sanctum.

From *Maharajah of the Movies*

Their first encounter was brief. Lilienthal stared at Marshall as she gracefully traversed his vast expanse of expensive carpet. Introductions were made. "So you're Erik's wonder girl," he growled, grasping her hand in his paw. "Take a seat. Tell me the story of your life."

As Marshall spoke, Lilienthal listened intently, his eyes rarely leaving her face. When she finished, the mogul sighed faintly. "Miss Marshall reminds me of Ida," he told Von Sternberg. "She's got that same—thing."

GEORGIA JAMES

From *Hollywood Talks*

You never heard of Ida Best? No, I guess not. She came and went so fast. Besides, people today know zilch about silent pictures. Stars like Colleen Moore, William Haines, Pola Negri were huge celebrities in their day, but who gives a flip for them now?

Ida Best was even bigger. They called her "The Too-Beautiful Girl." Old-timers say she was as wild as she was talented. Came out of nowhere in the early twenties. One of those overnight Broadway stars.

Somehow Lilienthal sweet-talked Ida into making pictures for Monolithic.

She was the first prestige name the place ever had. Before Ida came along, Monolithic was your basic custard pies and Westerns. But Ida gave the studio some class and also made them tons of money.

Rumor had it that Lilienthal was madly in love with her. Well, take a number.

Ida proved to be even bigger in early talkies. Then at the height of her career, she just disappeared. One fine day in 1929, Ida sailed off in her red little boat, bound for a weekend in Catalina, and never returned. Did she drown? Or was being a movie star getting to be too much for her, and she skipped? No one knows. The only thing for certain was that Ida was never heard from again. And all of Lilienthal's sweet dreams about Ida vanished into the blue with her.

When I first joined Monolithic's writing staff in 1933, there was an entire file cabinet of potential properties marked "Best." Plays, novels, stories. I thought that "Best" meant they were the likeliest future projects we owned. But no. Those were all the projects that Lilienthal was once going to make for Ida Best.

Soon after, I got hot about adapting one of them, an old Trollope novel titled *Kept in the Dark,* into a Janet Gaynor vehicle. Lilienthal shot that idea down right away, screaming, "That was Ida's!"

The next day, the file cabinet was gone.

Erik von Sternberg

From Eye for Beauty

I had won, but only up to a point.

As successful as Gene's interview with Lilienthal went, he was adamant about her tests. Shooting *Blonde Lace* was to be my only priority. "Anyway, if the girl is that good," he decreed, "she doesn't need all the little tricks you'll want to play with your camera."

Reluctantly, I surrendered my prize over to studio hands while resolving to make test footage of Gene secretly whenever I could steal a few moments.

Blonde Lace resumed the next day. Madra was surprisingly cooperative on the set, making no mention about events in New York. There was a steely professionalism about Madra that always stood her in good stead. She knew perfectly well that Gene was being tested for the flower girl role, but apparently had decided to wait and see what those results would be before making trouble.

So instead, Madra concentrated on playing Vera, the nightclub owner bothered by a gambling syndicate. Whatever threat she may have felt that Gene posed only caused Madra to perform with greater responsiveness to my direction. During the next week, while filming a long, sensual scene of seduction between Vera and Steve (the detective played by Trent Osborn), Madra acted with consummate charm and artistry.

When I complimented her after filming one particularly striking moment, she said, "I'm glad you feel that an old war horse like me still has a race or two left in her."

INTEROFFICE MEMOS

TO: Mr. Westland, Makeup Department

FROM: Mr. Lilienthal

DATE: Feb 25, 1941

RE: MISS GENE MARSHALL

Miss Marshall reports to you at 6:30 a.m. tomorrow to commence usual possible contractee makeup tests. Fix her up yourself. Do not cut her hair or make permanent alterations.

TO: Mr. Prinz

FROM: Mr. Lilienthal

DATE: Feb 25, 1941

RE: MISS GENE MARSHALL

Be at my office 10:30 a.m. tomorrow to discuss directing screen tests for Miss Marshall.

TED WESTLAND

Former director of Monolithic's makeup department

From *Hollywood Talks*

Even the most beautiful girls in Hollywood needed our skills.

Roz Russell once said, "It is miraculous how you unsung heroes make us actresses look—like we don't." Boy, she got that right.

When they first started out here, Crawford and Dietrich had to go on crash diets. We capped Alice Faye's teeth. Gave Sonja Henie her dimple. Poor Rita Hayworth's hairline and eyebrows were practically one and the same until we put her through electrolysis and managed to dig her out a forehead.

On the other hand, when Gene Marshall first walked into the makeup department, it was obvious there was little to do. Going in, she looked better than most girls coming out. In any event, Lilienthal said he liked Gene just fine the way she was, and Von Sternberg screamed he'd burn the place down if we tried anything drastic.

Mostly we experimented with finding a flattering makeup base. The new panchromatic makeup was just coming into use and suited her beautifully. All we did otherwise was a little plucking around her eyebrows, to shape them better.

But that was her as Gene Marshall, you understand.

You see, it was also customary in those days to experiment with unknowns to see what they looked like as other stars. That gave the studio some notion of the range of different roles they might play. We had all the wigs, putty, and makeup to do anything we wanted. Say, give me time and I can make King Kong look like Shirley Temple.

Anyway, we redid Gene as Dottie Lamour, Judy Garland, and several other reigning box-office champs of 1941. We shot both stills and moving footage to document what we did.

She was awfully good about it, never complained, although she nearly lost a layer of skin from the constant friction of putting on and taking off acres of makeup. Sometimes Gene was so quiet as we worked, it was almost like dressing up a doll.

CHARLIE BEAUCHAMP
Director of photography
From ASF's Oral History Project

I wasn't available to work on *Blonde Lace* since I was doing another picture when it first began shooting. But I was free by the time they needed tests run on Gene. The studio was in a big rush, because there was so much publicity over the girl; and they were hoping to cash in by giving her a part in *Blonde Lace,* which was already underway.

The makeup and makeover footage was routine. No need for fancy lighting. But it gave me an opportunity to study Gene's face and how it absorbed and reflected the light. Funny thing about the camera. Sometimes a raving beauty doesn't register on film. All sorts of Broadway lovelies all but broke the lens. Then you'd have to use special filters and shoot through layers of gauze to make them look human. The gag about Tallulah Bankhead during her Paramount years was that they had to shoot her through linoleum.

Gene presented us with few problems. Once we determined that a north light effect would best define her cheekbones and bring out the sparkle in her eyes, we had it made. Later, Von Sternberg liked to fiddle with her sidelighting, but it wasn't necessary.

Meanwhile, Gene was eager to learn about what we did on the other side of the camera. She never stopped with the questions. What did that piece of equipment do? What were the differences between the various diffusing lenses? Between shots, she'd walk around and talk to the grips and carpenters, who were thrilled to tell her about their jobs. I was glad to explain things myself. Too many actors believe that all they have to do is act and the rest happens by itself.

IVY JORDAN

From the minute Gene arrived on the lot, she hit the ground running. Two days after, they had determined what she'd do to prove whether she could act. One test scene would be for drama; the other, comedy. For the heavy-breathing stuff, they used the big telephone scene from *Infidelity*, one of Madra's early hits. The comedy was a goofy Thelma Todd–Patsy Kelly bit in a bakery that ends up with pie all over the place. Erik was beside himself. "Gene is a lady," he ranted. "She should be doing Portia's scene with her suitors, not this nonsense!"

"Anybody can do that artsy-craftsy Shakespeare stuff," said the boss. "I want to see how good the kid still looks with a blueberry pie in her kisser."

Then Rubi sent down word that I should do the other part in the bakery scene. It was a ten-minute bit about a society girl—Gene—who orders a birthday cake from a know-it-all baker—that was me—which tit-for-tat builds into a crazy mess in the kitchen.

Slapstick only looks easy, and I figured Gene needed pointers. I'm a local gal, you know, born and bred, and my family worked in one way or another at most of the studios; so I knew a lot of old-timers. I got hold of Buster Keaton and Mack Sennett, who were all washed up in movies by then but still knew their funny business better than anybody. They agreed to come over to teach a pretty newcomer a thing or three about comedy.

On Gene's Sunday off, the four of us tackled the scene in my backyard. Gene was hesitant at first, but with Buster showing her how to heft a pie and Sennett telling her the ways Mabel Normand handled knockabout farce, she rose to the occasion like you wouldn't believe.

By the end of the day, there were gobs of custard and whipped cream all over everything. Especially us. But Gene had an education. Mack and Buster had some fun. As for me, I had neighborhood cats, dogs, kids, and somebody's pet leopard in my yard for days afterward.

ERIK VON STERNBERG
From *Eye for Beauty*

Utter secrecy was essential.

I had no control over Gene's screen tests, but I was determined to help her. The stupid comedy scene she had to do was beyond my ken, but at least I was able to steal some time alone with Gene to rehearse her *Infidelity* sequence.

I was also making private tests that Lilienthal need not see until the proper time. We filmed late at night, after most of the studio personnel had left. I swore crew members to silence and paid them out of my own pocket. We used a bare minimum of lighting and shot the tests on the nightclub set. I had the film developed outside of the studio laboratory.

Most of the time I was content to film without sound. There was something haunting about Gene's appearance that silence enhanced.

IVY JORDAN

We did the comedy scene first. Our director was Roland Prinz, notorious around the lot as the "Prince of Prints," since he usually printed the very first take whether it was any good or not. If Rubi had deliberately tagged the biggest hack for Gene's testing, Prinz was the guy for it.

Lucky for us we had rehearsed ourselves, since Prinz was no help. He made us dry-run through it just once without using any props, and then he filmed the scene without a break. Well, it was hysterical. I was rarin' to go, and Gene matched me the entire way. We girls covered ourselves with glory, if I do say so myself. And about a ton of bakery-type goo. The only problem was that the sound track was spotty, because the crew kept laughing so hard at our antics.

The next day, Gene did her *Infidelity* scene. I went down to the set to keep her company and saw what happened. It was a difficult bit to do, since it was just Gene talking on the telephone in a close-up. The sequence involves a woman learning over the telephone that her husband is cheating on her. It starts out light and chatty and then goes into slow dawning, shock, and finally fighting back tears. Concluding in a breakdown after she hangs up. Now let me tell you that this is hardly an easy range of emotions even for an experienced actress, especially when it's just you and a dummy telephone.

Gene was terribly nervous, Prinz was in a hurry, and she just couldn't breathe life into it. She was stiff and amateurish, and there was zero magic. Everyone could tell Gene was unhappy with her performance, but Prinz decided to print the scene anyway.

Then Charlie informed Prinz about a technical glitch and how they'd have to do it over again after lunch. Gene was relieved to get another crack at the scene. "That's the nice thing about movies," Charlie told her.

I quickly put in a mayday call to Erik and, fortunately, he was able to sneak some time alone with Gene in her dressing room. Whatever Erik said to Gene accomplished wonders, since she marched right back to the telephone and did that scene brilliantly. Better than Madra's original, I thought, and that was a bit of acting that put Madra on the map early in her career.

CHARLIE BEAUCHAMP
From ASF's Oral History Project

It's more than fifty years ago, so I guess I can tell this story now.

We all saw that Gene had no help from the Prince of Prints. Poor kid hadn't a chance. Maybe if Von Sternberg had been on the set, things would be better, but that was impossible since he wasn't allowed near her. We figured that the big boss wanted to see how well Gene could function as an actress without her Svengali. Still, it didn't seem right.

Watching Gene struggle through the scene, you could see the guys shaking their heads in frustration. Gene had already made a number of friends among the crew, and we were feeling protective. But what could we do?

When she finished, I told Prinz that we had a problem with the camera and would have to shoot the scene again. I figured that Gene might be better on the second try.

Then after we broke for lunch, a couple of the recording guys came up to me with an idea. I sneaked over to the other stage where Von Sternberg was working and laid it out for him.

What we did was rig things up back on our set so that the telephone was really wired. Get it? On the other end of the line was Von Sternberg. So on the second take, all the time Gene was acting out the scene, Von Sternberg was coaching her through it over the telephone from his office.

From *Maharajah of the Movies*

Lilienthal made the projectionist run both tests repeatedly. He couldn't believe his eyes. Although the comedy scene was priceless, the high-charged emotional power that the neophyte displayed in her *Infidelity* sequence took his breath away.

Hours later, having summoned Marshall's lawyer Edward Ames to his office, Lilienthal could not believe his ears. Ames politely refused a seven-year studio pact.

"Dr. Marshall would never forgive me if I permitted his daughter to commit to anything for so long a period," explained Ames, proposing a one-picture deal.

Much as Lilienthal protested that unknown girls didn't dictate such terms, Ames refused to budge. "I scarcely think Miss Marshall is one whom you would accurately call an unknown," observed the sharp Yankee lawyer.

The mogul was about to order Ames out of his office when, as legend has it, his eye caught a glimpse of a portrait of Ida Best on the wall. Abruptly, he conceded to the lawyer's conditions.

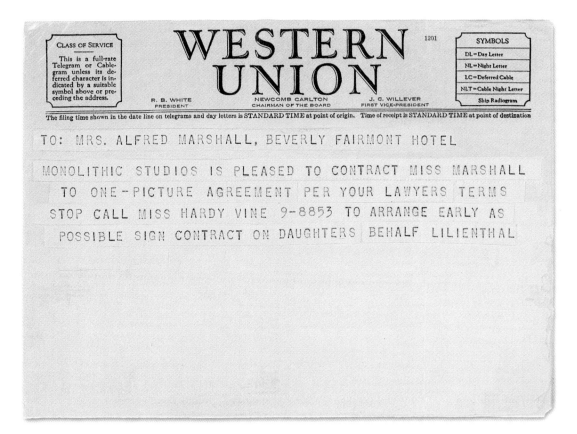

CLASS OF SERVICE

This is a full-rate Telegram or Cablegram unless its deferred character is indicated by a suitable symbol above or preceding the address.

R. B. WHITE
PRESIDENT

NEWCOMB CARLTON
CHAIRMAN OF THE BOARD

J. C. WILLEVER
FIRST VICE-PRESIDENT

1201

SYMBOLS

DL=Day Letter

NL=Night Letter

LC=Deferred Cable

NLT=Cable Night Letter

Ship Radiogram

The filing time shown in the date line on telegrams and day letters is STANDARD TIME at point of origin. Time of receipt is STANDARD TIME at point of destination

TO: MRS. ALFRED MARSHALL, BEVERLY FAIRMONT HOTEL

MONOLITHIC STUDIOS IS PLEASED TO CONTRACT MISS MARSHALL
TO ONE-PICTURE AGREEMENT PER YOUR LAWYERS TERMS
STOP CALL MISS HARDY VINE 9-8853 TO ARRANGE EARLY AS
POSSIBLE SIGN CONTRACT ON DAUGHTERS BEHALF LILIENTHAL

INTEROFFICE MEMOS

TO: Mr. Von Sternberg

FROM: Mr. Lilienthal

DATE: March 8, 1941

RE: GENE MARSHALL

All right, we've got your angel. She better be worth the fortune we're paying her.

TO: Miss James, Script Department

FROM: Mr. Lilienthal

DATE: March 8, 1941

RE: "BLONDE LACE"

Proceed with scene in nightclub checkroom for characters of Jane, Marjorie, and Steve. Make it hilarious.

TO: Miss Draper, Wardrobe Department

FROM: Mr. Lilienthal

DATE: March 8, 1941

RE: "BLONDE LACE"

Miss Gene Marshall has been assigned the flower girl role and reports to Wardrobe for fittings tomorrow morning. Requires your personal supervision. Mr. Von Sternberg will also speak to you later regarding needs for additional costumes.

TO: Mr. Axelrod, Studio Manager

FROM: Mr. Lilienthal

DATE: March 8, 1941

RE: GENE MARSHALL

Assign Miss Marshall a contract player's dressing room. One of the big ones. Make certain it is freshly painted and carpeted by noon yesterday.

TO: Miss Marshall

FROM: Mr. Lilienthal

DATE: March 8, 1941

RE: COSTUME FITTINGS

Kindly report to the Wardrobe Department tomorrow at 7 a.m. for costume fittings for "Blonde Lace."

9

"Blonde Lace"

CORA HARPER

From *Non-Stop Hollywood* syndicated column

Los Angeles Ledger

NON-STOP HOLLYWOOD

CHARMING NEW ENG-LAND MATRON MRS. ALFRED MARSHALL was swept off to Monolithic Pictures yesterday, where she signed a contract on behalf of her daughter Gene—still a minor—for a role in "Blonde Lace." Afterward, Mrs. Marshall was treated to a celebratory luncheon at the Green Parrot by several leading lights of Motion Picture Mothers, Inc. The devoted mamas of Tyrone Power, Gary Cooper, Ann Sothern, and Loretta Young welcomed Mrs. Marshall into their fold as the newest member of their worthy charitable organization.

As the lovely Gene prepares to step before the cameras this week, it's said that her role as a cigarette girl is being expanded. A little green birdie says that studio execs were overwhelmed by Gene's tests and intend to make greater use of her talents in the picture.

RKO HOPES TO BUY the latest Rodgers & Hart hit "Pal Joey" for Irene Dunne and John Payne if the censors allow

BENNY MAJORS

I wasn't surprised when Madra invited me over to see Gene's screen tests. Madra had a personal spy system at Monolithic second to nobody and got her mitts on them with no problem. She ran the tests at home in her living room. A tapestry went up, there was the screen, and her butler ran the projector.

Madra was silent through the comedy scene, finally smacking me when I started howling as those two girls fell into this enormous birthday cake. "The kid's pretty good," I said. "I suppose she's all right," snapped Madra. "If you like that vulgar sort of thing."

It was Madra's turn to laugh when we screened the next test. Marshall was a gorgeous girl, no doubt, but it was clear she had no idea what she was doing with Madra's famous telephone scene. Amateur night. Madra got a big kick out of seeing Gene sweat through it.

"Can you believe they'd sign a girl who can't act?" she said. "Rubi is out of his mind."

"She's awfully pretty," I cautioned her. "Good looks like that go a long way."

"Not far enough," said Madra, looking pleased. "I'll wipe up the floor with her."

Of course, later I found out that there was a second telephone test we hadn't known about. But by that time it was a totally different ball game.

HARRY HALE
From ASF's Oral History Project

Just as the initial newspaper and radio excitement over Gene's discovery died down, the weeklies hit, and another huge wave of interest swelled up. Requests for interviews flooded us.

The boss told me to say no to everything. "We're not sure what we've got here," he said about Gene. "So it's best we keep her under wraps for a while. A little mystery never hurt a rising star." But he instructed me to keep Gene busy in the portrait gallery so we could at least keep the press happy with plenty of photos.

"We're going to need to dress her up," I told him.

"Why do we have all these warehouses full of clothes?" he said. "You tell the boys to use anything they want." But he ordered me to keep a close eye on their work. No cheesecake!

We photographed her alone and with practically every star on the lot. In a sunbonnet with Happy Trales. In yellow gingham, baking cookies for the Bratzanjammer Boys. In costumes for every month of the year for a 1942 calendar going out to our exhibitors. The animation department boys even fixed her up with Minky Doodle Dandy draped over her shoulders.

I also had to be concerned for Gene's safety. Celebrities enjoyed more privacy than they do now, but all too many strangers were itchy to get near Gene. The Beverly Fairmont had a top-notch security force, and a studio car took Gene back and forth every day. I also hired an ex-prizefighter, Slapsie Harris, to stick by her side in public. Of course, those first months, Gene didn't see anything but the inside of the studio.

ERIK VON STERNBERG

From *Eye for Beauty*

Discretion often is a simple matter of timing.

There was no need to hurl Gene immediately into her scripted exchange with Madra. Before their confrontation, I thought it best that Gene should experience a few days of filming where she wouldn't be in the spotlight.

Like most pictures, *Blonde Lace* was not being shot in chronological order. So thanks to our schedule, I could slip Gene into the picture unobtrusively.

We were filming incidents showing the Panda Club in all of its nighttime glamour. They were among the opening scenes, as the detective initially visits the club and encounters Madra's character. Several dozen dress extras were employed as black-tie patrons, along with others dressed as the staff.

As Marjorie, the flower girl, Gene would first be glimpsed as a figure in the background, selling her high-priced posies to the customers. With the camera angles and detailed atmosphere I planned, it would take several days before Gene and Madra actually filmed their face-off.

In the meantime, both Madra and Gene would be on the set together as part of the general nightclub sequence. So much the better, I thought. Let them get acquainted.

ELLIE DRAPER
Former Monolithic wardrobe director
From Suzanne Hershey's *Designers on Design*
(New York: Entertainment Technology Press, 1988)

When we were planning the clothes for *Blonde Lace,* Erik came up with his flower girl notion. A sweeter image than the usual cigarette girl, he thought. Practically speaking, it amounted to much the same thing. A short bouffant skirt in chartreuse satin with a pink petticoat, white organdy apron, a decorative little tray with straps to go over bare shoulders. Once I had Gene in the shop, it was an easy costume to whip together.

At the same time Gene arrived, orders came down from the front office that her character required more clothes. The sort of things that a nice college girl might wear on a rainy evening. Coat, sweater and skirt, hat, some pretty underclothes, too, for a changing scene.

GEORGIA JAMES
From *Hollywood Talks*

After okaying a draft of the checkroom scene, Erik started me on something fresh. This sequence would show Gene getting off a streetcar, walking down a gloomy alley into the club's employee entrance, and then going through the joint to a dressing room where she'd change clothes among the showgirls.

It was mostly a silent bit for Gene; just a few friendly hellos. The idea of a butterfly coming out of a cocoon, explained Erik.

Yes, and a nifty way to garner Gene some extra time on-screen, which was fine by me. Well, well, I thought, let's see how Erik finesses this clever idea around Miss Madra.

Ivy Jordan

For good luck, I drove Gene to the studio for her first day of shooting. We were in makeup and hair by the crack of dawn and ready to go by eight. We got to the nightclub set on Stage Four before anyone else in the cast. Technicians were busy lighting the set for the opening setup.

Gene explored the setting while I got to gabbing with Trent, who was doing all those nightclub scenes with us. Remember? I give him a hard time when he tries to check in his dirty old trench coat with me. Anyway, when I next looked for Gene she was on the other side of the set gazing up at the Panda Club staircase.

A tremendous thing, if you recall the movie. These broad marble stairs leading up to a thirty-foot-high black glass and white plaster whatzit with all this crazy scrollwork. A doorway cut into the middle of it. In some odd way, it looked especially imposing rising up in the middle of the soundstage. Some weird whale beached amid all the lighting rigs and camera equipment.

Gene slowly walked up the staircase and peered into the darkness on the other side of the door. I'll always remember watching that. She reminded me of Alice in Wonderland or the girl in the red shoes or one of those fairy-tale heroines who suddenly finds herself in a strange place full of exotic happenings. That was Gene in Hollywood, all right.

Then she came back down, smiling, practicing floating down the stairs without looking at her feet. She tried it several times more before we got into positions for the first take. As part of the action, Gene was instructed to glide down the stairs into the crowd. We ran it through twice, and then got ready to make the scene.

I asked Gene if she was nervous. Not really, she said, as long as she knew where to go.

Alarm bells. Lights! Sound! Camera rolling! Action! Fifteen seconds of nightclub whoopee. Cut!

Erik pronounced himself satisfied—which was a miracle all by itself—and we moved on to the next setup.

Madra wasn't on call that day, so we had no worries there. We were shooting general atmosphere. The Panda Club "customers" laughed it up while we "employees" went about our business. I checked hats, Gene drifted around with her flower tray, and Erik rode the camera boom, swooping around to film our moves.

Gene Marshall

When we finished late that afternoon, I asked Gene if she liked making movies. She smiled and said, more than anything she'd ever done before in her life.

ERIK VON STERNBERG
From *Eye for Beauty*
The next morning's rushes were stunning.

The Panda Club's black-and-white decor, the gleaming glass and chandeliers, the glittering throng. Amid it all wandered Gene. Perfection.

Lilienthal was impressed. "That girl certainly does stand out in a crowd, doesn't she?" he marveled in the screening room. He knew as well as I that the lights were subtly keyed to pick out Gene's face, but even so, she projected a luminosity all her own.

By this time, I was beginning to understand her gifts. Gene wasn't yet someone who could calculate her effects. That would come later. For the moment, Gene was successfully relying upon her spontaneous ability to believe in what she was doing. Her mother often told me childhood stories of Gene pretending to be imaginary characters for days on end.

Once when we were making a picture, I asked Barbara Stanwyck what she felt was the basis of great film acting. "Just be truthful," she told me, "and if you can fake that, you've got it made." Gene wasn't yet experienced at faking anything. She was simply being truthful about who she was pretending to be.

Harry Hale
From ASF's Oral History Project

I was walking Gene back to the set from a portrait gallery session when she encountered Madra for the first time since New York. Ivy was with us, gabbing a mile a minute. Madra drove up to the soundstage and got out of a block-long Cadillac, attended by her maid, chauffeur, and agent. Ivy broke the ice, saying, "Madra, you remember Miss Marshall, don't you?"

"Who can ever possibly hope to forget her?" replied Madra.

Gene smiled and said she was glad to see Miss Lord again, too. She had been so busy ever since that night that she hadn't had a chance to thank her for being so nice at the premiere. Madra looked indulgent.

"I understand that you performed my telephone scene as a test," said Madra pleasantly enough. "I hope that your acting wasn't too affected by my original interpretation."

Gene explained that she wasn't influenced by Madra's performance. When *Infidelity* came out a few years before, her mother wouldn't allow her to see it.

Madra was amused. Why not? she wondered.

Gene blushed and confessed that her mother thought she was too young. Ivy howled.

Madra froze for a moment, then huffed off, her entourage chasing after.

GEORGIA JAMES
From *Hollywood Talks*

Surprisingly, Erik whipped through those busy Panda Club scenes with no sweat.

Lousing everything up though was a big floor show number. Orchestra, dance routine, the works. The deck consisted of these large checkerboard squares, which would lift up individually, so the chorus girls could pop through and sink back down again when the number was over. You know the song, right? "You Floor Me." Madra sang it.

Dubbed it, really, since Madra sang like a vulture. Synching the number was a pain: Madra had trouble matching her movements with the playback, and those squares in the floor kept popping up and down at all the wrong times.

While Madra was rehearsing with her dance coach, Erik took Gene and Ivy over to another soundstage and filmed their snappy checkroom encounter with Trent. One, two, three, quick as spit, and they were done in an afternoon. I know every inch of that scene and I still laugh whenever I see it. Watching the dailies, Lilienthal was so pleased by Gene's performance that he made a point of inviting her to one of his famous Sunday socials.

TRENT OSBORN
From *My Bed of Roses*

Once or twice a month, RL hosted these enormous Sunday brunches at his place out in Santa Monica. Half of Hollywood would be there. Plus everyone at Monolithic who was in RL's favor at the moment. It was almost medieval how you were expected to go out there to kiss the boss's ring. Only it wasn't his ring you kissed, if you catch my drift.

Actually, I never minded going, because RL laid out a marvelous spread of food and booze; and there was always plenty of pretty girls splashing around his pool. RL's place was huge, an estate really, with acres of terraced gardens, tennis courts, a perfectly manicured croquet lawn, skeet shooting, everything.

Madra was too occupied with being fitted for her gown for the Oscars that next week, so she stayed home. Erik brought his wife, Zena, which made it something of an occasion, since she rarely went out socially. "One of the nicest things about being in retirement is that I don't have to make these command appearances if I don't want to," she once told me. I guess Zena was there with Erik to spike the false rumors cropping up that Erik's relationship with Gene was more than merely professional.

"Erik always falls in love with his discoveries," Zena told me. "Really, it means nothing, since he only consummates his passion through the camera. Besides, I like the little Marshall girl. She reminds me of myself when I came out here from the old country."

RL's brunch marked the first time that Gene had ventured into Hollywood society. Between all those tests, her publicity photos, and working on the picture, the poor kid had been slaving away at the studio. So for Gene to find herself amid the likes of Norma Shearer, Dolores Del Rio, and Fred Astaire must've been astounding. Even I was impressed by the crowd RL got.

Gene was astonished to discover that most of the stars were eager to chat with the unknown who had caused such a cross-country sensation. "Hey, you, new-kid-in-town!" yelled Carole Lombard from across the patio, "come over here and meet poor Clark before he dies of curiosity!" Soon enough, Cesar Romero, Randy Scott, and a little band of Hollywood's best-known bachelors were buzzing around her.

Despite her warm welcome, Gene must have felt uncomfortable being around so many famous faces because she vanished. I gave up looking for her and got into the swim with the bathing beauties. In fact, that was the same afternoon I bumped into Hedy Lamarr underwater. To say the least, it proved to be quite an ecstatic first encounter.

From *Maharajah of the Movies*

Making his rounds as a host, Lilienthal came across Marshall on his croquet court. A posse of Hollywood's most expert players watched in wonderment as the young actress happily swept across the course, sending her opponents' croquet balls rocketing off into the distance.

"Look at that little girlie make that killer three-ball break," marveled Sam Goldwyn. "She's too pretty to play so tough."

When Lilienthal wondered how she entered the match, Marshall told him that she felt awkward among so many celebrities. But she loved croquet, and when she saw a game about to begin, she simply asked the players if she could join. She had no notion that they were some of the industry's top executives.

Lilienthal nodded thoughtfully and joined the growing crowd of onlookers. When Marshall finally emerged from the match, flushed and victorious, the mogul was grinning. "I just made five thousand dollars betting on you winning," he crowed. "Honey, you're the first person to ever make me money before completing a single picture. You can play for me anytime."

ALICE MARSHALL
From a letter to Dr. Marshall

...applauded when she won. Katie said that Sandy always told her that playing croquet was all in the shoulders.

We finally got out to Ned Ames's house for dinner last night. I had no idea they had be-come so well off. Louisa has put on weight, but she's as much a kidder as ever. Their children are sweet. Paul, the only boy, is in his junior year of college, very quiet and serious. I think he's a bit taken with our Katie. Not that he did much but sneak long peeks at her during dinner. Afterward, he insisted on driving us back.

You shouldn't worry about the expense of the hotel. The studio pays for everything as part of that contract that Ned worked out. I thought we might come home as early as next week, but VS says that Katie has done so well that extra scenes are being written for her, and so we should expect to be here awhile longer.

I don't like the idea of you being by yourself, dear, and I miss you dreadfully; but I can't leave Katie. As much as I sit around all day with nothing to do, I want to be here when Katie comes back at night. If I didn't insist, I don't think she'd eat a thing. She practically falls into bed the second she comes through the door.

Try to tune into the Academy Awards broadcast next Sunday. Katie is going! Mr. Lilienthal insists she join the Monolithic party. Katie bought the prettiest party dress with her first paycheck. She was so proud to be able to pay for it herself. VS will escort Katie, since Zena is expecting their next baby soon and is remaining at home. I'll be here by the radio. It will do my heart good knowing that you're listening in, too....

CORA HARPER
From *Non-Stop Hollywood* syndicated column

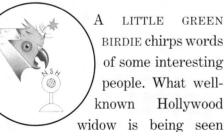

Los Angeles Ledger

NON-STOP HOLLYWOOD

A LITTLE GREEN BIRDIE chirps words of some interesting people. What well-known Hollywood widow is being seen lately with a dapper ladies' man who doesn't allow his wedding ring to keep him from the ladies? Which Western costars came to fisticuffs over their misleading lady while filming on location in Yuma? And which big female star is boiling over the extra attention a newcomer is receiving on the set of the picture they're making together?

BENNY MAJORS

After slaving like a dog over getting "You Floor Me" in the can, Madra went through the roof when she learned about the new scenes with Marshall. In no time flat, we were both in a powwow with Lilienthal. "I'm only thinking about the film," Madra kept insisting. "Those extra scenes only stall things. It will all end up on the cutting room floor. You never see her again after my character fires her, so what's with the big buildup?"

Lilienthal replied that there was so much advance publicity on Marshall that audiences would expect to see more. When Madra asked whether still more scenes for Marshall were planned, Lilienthal wouldn't give her an answer. "Let's just see how it goes," he said. When Madra declared that she had script approval in her contract, Lilienthal pointed out how the fine print stated that her approval pertained only to scenes in which she appeared. Madra was furious, of course, but the only person she could take it out on was me, since I had negotiated the deal. The screaming that went on afterward wasn't pretty, believe you me.

"I won't have that no-talent nobody steal a second picture from me," said Madra. "That kid is riding for a rude awakening."

IVY JORDAN

We called the Academy Awards that year the "surprise party." Because 1941 was the first time that the results were kept secret until the Price Waterhouse envelopes were opened on the podium. So everyone who was nominated was a wreck. They were all knocking back aspirin and tranquilizers. You never saw so many shades of green this side of a St. Patrick's Day parade.

Back in those days, the awards were given out during a banquet for about fifteen hundred people or so. There was even dancing between courses and some of the technical prizes. Monolithic had reserved two big tables for its stars and Oscar nominees. Madra had done *He Married His Boss* on loan to Paramount, but because she was the queen of our lot, she sat with us.

Bob Hope emceed, but the biggest laugh of the night happened before the awards started. Waltzing down the staircase into the Biltmore ballroom, poor Carole Landis lost her slip, which swaddled around her ankles. Everybody who saw it started howling. Unfortunately, all this happened just as Madra was making her big entrance, too, and she thought we were laughing at her. This did not put her into the best mood, and Madra sat there steaming all through President Roosevelt's radio address broadcast direct to us from Washington.

While Judy Garland was singing "America," I saw Madra pour herself a stiff drink from a flask she had stashed in her purse. From the way Madra kept fortifying herself all night long, it wouldn't have surprised me to learn that she had packed a couple of flasks. I don't blame her—the best actress awards weren't announced until the very end, and she was plenty jittery. Knowing how she was, everybody at the table tactfully left Madra alone, so she seethed in silence, crumbling up her breadsticks and every so often shooting ugly looks at Bette Davis and Joan Fontaine.

Gene, who was at the other Monolithic table with me, appeared to be in heaven as she stared at all the celebrities around her. She looked mighty heavenly, too, in a floral print with a beautiful white fox wrap that Erik had borrowed from the wardrobe department. Gene stayed as still as a mouse and politely said no to everyone who asked her to dance. I think it was the first time that any girl had ever turned down Robert Taylor for anything.

The boss had other ideas, though, and eventually he took Gene out for a spin on the dance floor. For a short guy, Rubi was a superb dancer, and he whirled Gene around the floor like nobody's business. When Louis B. Mayer tried to cut in, Rubi refused to let her go. For a second it looked like the heads of MGM and Monolithic were about to belt each other.

GEORGIA JAMES
From *Hollywood Talks*

Hell's bells, I remember that night all too well. I lost Best Original Screenplay to Preston Sturges. Johnny Shaw lost Best Song to "When You Wish Upon a Star." One by one, Mono's nominees got shot down. Vicky Steiner won for film editing, but who gave a flip?

By the time they got to the acting awards, we were mighty glum. Alfred Lunt and Lynn Fontanne were the presenters. Madra, who was deep into the moonshine by that time, snorted, "Who asked a couple of theater hams like them to give out our Oscars? They only made one lousy movie in their whole career, and it was a dog!"

Then, jumping Jerusalem, our own Dame Elinor Pomeroy wins Best Supporting Actress. The old girl must have been seventy-five if she was a minute, but she leaped for the stage like a jackrabbit, laughing, crying, giving a better performance than she did in her picture.

Now Madra must have thought that was a good sign, because while Walter Brennan and Jimmy Stewart were goshing and gawing and accepting their Oscars, she was halfway under the table, redoing her makeup. She popped back up, nose practically powdered blue, just as Lynn Fontanne started reading out the Best Actress nominees.

TRENT OSBORN
From *My Bed of Roses*

Miss Fontanne opened the envelope, drew a breath, and trilled, "My! The winner is Ginger Rogers!"

Well, in the split second Madra heard Miss Fontanne sound out the letter *M* in those rolling theatrical tones, she figured that she had beat out Bette, Joan, Kate, and Ginger and had sprung to her feet, all ready to accept her laurels. As the spotlight swept across the floor searching for Ginger, it hit Madra dead-on as she collapsed back into her seat, red as a fire engine. Fortunately for her, most people were eyeing Ginger, so only those of us near Madra saw.

IVY JORDAN

I almost split a gut to keep myself from laughing. Madra stared open-mouthed as Ginger, weeping buckets, thanked her mother. Then as the party broke up, Gene foolishly went over to Madra, who was still sitting there, and told her how sorry she was. "Who cares what you think," snapped Madra, waving her off. But as she did, Madra's hand smacked a glass, splattering Gene's gown with red wine. Big bloody spots of it.

Did Madra do that on purpose? I was too far away to tell. The boss came to his own conclusion, though. "You bitch," Rubi declared. "I saw what you did!" I don't know what he said to Madra after that, because I was hustling Gene off to the powder room to try to repair the damage.

Gene's sweet new dress was ruined, but she was a good sport, saying that Madra was probably too upset to know what she was doing. "Don't bet on it," I told her. When we finally came out, Rubi was waiting for us, holding out that fabulous white fox for Gene. "I want you to keep this," he said. Gene protested, but the boss was firm. "Yes," he insisted. "It's studio property, and what I say goes."

ERIK VON STERNBERG
From *Eye for Beauty*

Awards are meaningless to me. My work provides all the reward that I need.

For several days after the awards ceremony, Madra was reported as ill and did not work. I used the available time to film a new opening sequence when Gene's character arrives at the club.

Blonde Lace was coming together better than I had hoped. The script was still worrisome, but the nightclub scenes were extremely effective. Gene was responding miraculously to my direction. We enjoyed a tremendous rapport from the beginning, and every day she gained confidence. The scenes we constructed for Gene were easily accomplished. She was always pliant. Perceptive. And a pleasure. I felt that I could direct her forever.

I suggested to Lilienthal that we develop a subplot for Gene that extended her presence in the film. Impressed with the dailies, he assented, and Georgia was dispatched to her typewriter. But she had barely begun by the time Gene and Madra were slated to shoot their scene together.

Up to then, Madra had ignored Gene on the set. But that morning she approached Gene with a smile. "You may as well know that I'm not one of these actresses who breezes through a rehearsal," said Madra. "I give it my all, whether the camera is rolling or not, and I expect you to do the same." Gene nodded and took her place in the middle of the stairs. I directed her to descend, brush into Madra, and begin their dialogue from there.

They started rehearsal. Halfway through it, right after Gene offered a flower from her tray, Madra brushed it aside and slapped Gene, who stepped back in confusion.

"What are you doing?" I screamed.

"Improvising," said Madra, looking innocent. "I thought my character should do something like that."

"That's wrong," I told her. "Vera may be hard-boiled, but no matter how angry she was, she'd hardly hit the girl in front of all those people." The makeup crew hovered around Gene, fussing over the red mark that Madra's hand left on her cheek. Gene insisted she was ready to rehearse again.

They returned to their marks and began the scene afresh. Again Madra slapped Gene. Even harder than before. This time Gene fled the set.

"Sometimes a character simply takes over me," proclaimed Madra to no one in particular. "I just don't know what I'm doing."

10

Falling Star

From *Maharajah of the Movies*

Word of the slapping incident brought Lilienthal thundering to the stage. The crew was darkly muttering up in the rafters. Von Sternberg fumed. Lord was smoking a cigarette, tilted back on her reclining board. Marshall stood distant from the others, an ice pack on her cheek and a withdrawn expression on her face.

Lilienthal strategically straightened out the chaos. Lord refused to apologize, insisting the slap "seemed like the right thing to do at the time," but swore to forgo it in the future. Von Sternberg was placated by a quiet promise that Marshall's role would continue to be enhanced. Marshall was treated to a fatherly lunch in the executive dining room as Lilienthal outlined technicolor plans for her career.

When Marshall returned to her dressing room, she discovered it packed with flowers. There were lilies from Lilienthal, violets from Von Sternberg, and an entire azalea bush that crew members had lifted off the nearby set of *Forever Spring*. There was also a sheaf of gladiolas from Lord, whose card read, "Here's to your first big hit, kid."

Under Lilienthal's stern supervision, the brief scene was filmed from several angles without further incident. Both actresses went through their paces smoothly, but wordlessly retreated to opposite corners between setups. Tomorrow, Von Sternberg announced with relief, they would film the scene again in a long shot to complete the sequence.

CORA HARPER

From *Luncheon with the Stars* radio broadcast

```
                         --CORA HARPER: Tell us, Myrna, is it true that
                      after you finish "Shadow of the Thin Man," it will
                      be your final picture in the series?
                         --MYRNA LOY: Who can say? I adore working with
                      William Powell, of course, and—
                         --CORA HARPER: What, Tommy? Excuse me—I've
                      just been handed this—oh, dear—
                         --MYRNA LOY: What ever's the matter, Cora?
                         --CORA HARPER: Well, it seems there's just
                      been some sort of accident over at Monolithic on
                      the set of "Blonde Lace" . . .
                  --MYRNA LOY: That picture with Madra Lord and the lovely new girl?
                  --CORA HARPER: Mm-hm. I have only the sketchiest report here. Appar-
                  ently a set collapsed or something. Ambulances were arriving, and the fire
                  department, too.
                     --MYRNA LOY: That doesn't sound good.
                     --CORA HARPER: Well, we'll try to get listeners further details be-
                  fore we finish today's Luncheon with the Stars. My guest today at the Green
                  Parrot is the charming Myrna Loy. You once made a picture with Madra, did-
                  n't you, Myrna?
                     --MYRNA LOY: Yes, I did. A few years ago. I played the other woman in
                  "Infidelity."
                     --CORA HARPER: What was working with Madra like?
                     --MYRNA LOY: Well, let's just say it was a different experience than
                  working with Bill Powell.
```

IVY JORDAN

I've been asked again and again about the accident. I saw it happen with my own
eyes, twenty feet away, but even then it seemed like a dream. No, a nightmare.

The day before had been lousy enough with that slapping business. Sure, we
knew Madra could make trouble on a set, but she'd never actually slugged somebody
before. It finally wised up Gene, though, who at last saw Madra for what she was.

That morning, as Gene took up her flower tray, she told me Rubi had promised that Madra wouldn't bother her again. "You better believe she won't," said the prop guy, nodding.

There were visitors on the set that day, I forget who or from where they were, but we all became extra professional in front of strangers.

Everyone got into position for the long shot. A dozen or so extras, Trent at a table, me at the checkroom window—I was in real long shot, brother—and Madra about to cross the dance floor. Gene was midway up the stairs. The boom, with Erik and the camera operator, slowly rose high into position.

Ready? Lights, camera, action. Gene descends the stairs and brushes into Madra. They launch into the scene. All's going well, and then, suddenly, Madra isn't there anymore. Just a long, drawn-out shriek.

MADRA LORD
From *Dark Radiance*

Without warning, the floor gave way beneath me. My career—my very life!—hung in the balance for one eternal millisecond. Then all was darkness.

GEORGIA JAMES
From *Hollywood Talks*

I finally believed in God when I saw the earth open up and swallow Madra. She just dropped out of sight. Gone in a flash like a devil sent back to Hell. Nobody else moved.

TRENT OSBORN
From *My Bed of Roses*

My back was halfway turned so all I knew was that Madra screamed. By the time I whipped around, she had vanished. But the scream kept going on and on. Gene looked like the most startled thing on earth, staring down at this hole where Madra had been standing. I don't know how long we were all transfixed like that—it seemed like forever—and then everyone rushed toward the spot.

ERIK VON STERNBERG

From *Eye for Beauty*

Madra's plunge was one of the most striking things I ever witnessed.

From my god's-eye point of view atop the camera boom, the sudden frenzy of movement as people raced across the black-and-white floor provided a stunning mosaic of humanity. In the center of the broiling mob, there stood Gene, frozen with shock.

JIMMY MORRISON

Camera operator

From *Hollywood Talks*

Somehow, we kept on filming. "Get a closeup," ordered Von Sternberg. "Closer, closer," he kept saying until I told him that we were practically back down on the

floor. We got it all. The crowd, Gene's startled face, and finally this gap in the checkerboard next to Gene's feet. By that time we were so low that we only had to step off the boom onto the deck, where everyone was desperately trying to get a peek down below.

IVY JORDAN

For one split second, nobody budged. Then everything happened very, very fast. Everyone tore around like maniacs. As if life were trying to catch up with the beat it had just missed. Madra's stylish chapeau was our only clue that she had been there a moment before. But wherever she'd gone, you sure could hear her. The shriek turned into these unearthly muffled noises from below.

The nightclub set had traps built into it for the chorus girls doing the "You Floor Me" number. And one of the panels gave way. Madra tumbled right through to the soundstage basement a dozen feet below. Why she didn't sue Monolithic for plenty I never could figure. Maybe she was just glad to come out of it alive.

PETE SEAVER
Former Monolithic stagehand

Yeah, I was the first one to reach Madra after it happened. It was easy for me to swing through the trap and drop down. The basement was concrete, but Madra had landed in a heap of old burlap sacks that broke her fall. Maybe saved her life, even. She was all tangled up in them, spitting and cursing a blue streak.

When I got over to her, she looked at me like I was going to murder her and started fighting me off. "Hey, I'm on your side," I told her.

I was, too. Years before, we'd gotten real close for a little while when she was still working her way up. After she became a big star, Madra had always been good to me and a couple of the other boys she knew from her early days on the lot.

Finally, she recognized me and began screeching that her ankle was busted. "Who did this to me?" she kept moaning as we waited together for the ambulance.

BRUCE BALDWIN

From *Hollywood Gomorrah* (New York: Venus Publishing, 1995)

Was it purely an accident? Or a deliberate attempt to dim a shining star?

Marshall had stood on the same fatal square only scant seconds before Lord set foot on it. Perhaps the accident was meant to befall Marshall. Lord, threatened by the newcomer's popularity, may well have slyly engineered the incident with a favored member of the crew, only to fall into a pit of her own design. The fact that the tempestuous star never sued the studio and subsequently cooperated with the completion of the film suggests that Lord may have had a guilty conscience.

FALLING STAR!

MONOLITHIC'S MINXIE MADRA LORD took a dive on the set of *Blonde Lace* this afternoon. Our exclusive sources report that Lord's accidental downfall means a major turn up in the career of Gene Marshall, the newly-discovered

But if the accident was intended for Lord, who might have been responsible?

When much of the Monolithic lot was demolished for a shopping mall in the 1970s, a primitive network of secret listening devices was uncovered, wired directly into the former offices of studio founder Reuben Lilienthal. Although it is unlikely that he would risk injuring a valuable studio asset like Lord, it is conceivable that Lilienthal became aware of Lord's scheme to harm Marshall and had reversed the situation with the aid of loyal staff.

With his own agenda and minions to assist him in a scheme to replace Lord with Marshall, eccentric director Erik von Sternberg is another key figure who may have had a clandestine hand in the mishap.

Or perhaps a few of the crew may have quietly taken it upon themselves to punish Lord for striking out at Marshall on the previous day. The rising young star had endeared herself to the technicians, many of whom had endured Lord's volatile temperament for years.

Then again, the mysterious calamity that laid low one of Hollywood's biggest names on that day in March 1941 may simply have been one of those Tinseltown strokes of fate that leads to the rise—or in this case, fall—of the stars.

ALICE MARSHALL
From a letter to Dr. Marshall

…why she had come back from the studio so early, she said there had been an accident. Madra Lord had broken her leg. After what that creature did to Katie yesterday, I'm afraid that I'm not very Christian in thinking that it couldn't happen to a more deserving person. Honestly, I could have pushed her myself.

You know how Katie gets when she's upset. Very quiet. She spent the rest of the afternoon in the pool, swimming back and forth without stopping until she was exhausted. After supper, just when I was trying to get Katie to go to bed, a call came that a car was being sent to take her back to the studio. It's near midnight, so heaven only knows what they're up to now over there. The longer we stay here, the crazier this place seems to me.

Harry Hale
From ASF's Oral History Project

The doctors said it was a compound fracture and that it would be at least a month before Madra would be able to work in front of the cameras.

Lilienthal immediately called a conference. He said there was no way that *Blonde Lace* could be postponed until Madra was able to return. He couldn't tie up the cast and crew waiting for her. He also said the picture was too far advanced to redo from scratch with another leading lady. So he felt forced to scrap the entire thing. Insurance would cover some costs, but the studio was going to take a terrible bath anyway, having invested a lot of moola. Still, the boss saw no alternative unless anyone had some other idea.

At that point, Erik and Georgia jumped up and practically kidnapped Lilienthal, hauling him into the screening room to look at the existing pieces of the movie.

Georgia James
From *Hollywood Talks*

When the accident happened, maybe one-quarter of *Blonde Lace* was in the can. All this ultra glamorous business of the club in full swing, including the "You Floor Me" number. A long, smoky encounter between Steve and Vera in the penthouse. Gangsters threatening Vera. Ivy being flip. The new opening as Gene's character, Marjorie, slips into the club. Various takes of that nasty little business between Vera and Marjorie.

Oh, and the accident footage. We all wanted to see that. As the lab rushed it through, Erik ran all the tests he and Charlie Beauchamp had secretly made of Gene. They were mostly silent, filmed on the set of the club with very little lighting. A string of variations on this mysterious beauty reposing in a huge shadowy never-never land. Lounging at a table. Floating up and down the stairs. Drifting across the room. Darkness always lurking round the edges.

The contrast in mood between Gene's tests and all the other footage was amazing. Night and day. Finally we screened the accident. It began with a long shot angled from high above the nightclub, panning down toward Madra and Gene. Then Madra drops from view, and the camera zooms in toward Gene's face, looking incredibly beautiful and incredibly shocked as the extras converged upon her. We ran it a couple of times. There was a hallucinatory quality about it.

"God, I wish we could use that moment," groaned Lilienthal when the sequence flickered out. "Such an unexpected thing, coming after all that nightclub business."

Maybe we can, said Erik. "Danger within such glamorous illusion is fascinating, is it not?"

Lilienthal looked puzzled. Eric started talking—words flying—making up an entire new scenario for the picture. One that would use most of what had been shot so far, including Madra's scenes, and incorporating some of Gene's tests. A picture making Gene the leading character.

Erik had this notion that *Blonde Lace* could be reconfigured as a thriller. One that contrasted glamour with darkness. You know, sometimes things would look incredibly lovely, but always behind the glitter there'd be terrible, unexpected danger lurking. Erik's spiel set off bells for me, and soon I was pitching rewrite ideas.

Vera's husband, the one who had keeled over from a bum ticker, could be made into a murder victim. And now we'd kill Vera off about half an hour into things. That would shock the audience no end, since in those days you expected a big star like Madra to last through the whole picture.

Gene's character could in fact be the dead club owner's long-lost daughter, who inherits the club after Vera croaks. That would put her in the hot spot. Then I came up with the notion that we never finger exactly who done it. The gangster stuff would be a red herring. So anyone might die. The audience would not know which way to look.

Of course, risking a major feature on the talents of a novice like Gene was a scary proposition. But Gene had performed magically so far under Eric's guidance, so why couldn't he pull it out of her? Erik suggested that we'd give Gene's character very little to say. Enigmatic, you know? It added mystery, and minimal dialogue would make Gene's acting job easier.

Sure, I joked, and let's make her a sleepwalker, too.

Erik looked at me. Hard. "That's a wonderful idea," he said.

Lilienthal drank it in, lit a cigar, and pondered. He'd taken bigger risks. Like the time he jumped into making talking pictures when everyone else believed them a fad. His daring had transformed Monolithic into the industry giant it was today.

Georgia James

"Well, why not?" he decided, smacking the top of his desk.

Suddenly we were back in business. Doing something completely new. They didn't have a name for it just then, but out of the wreckage of a lame-brained comedy called *Blonde Lace* we started making a film noir.

11

Tale Spin

CORA HARPER

From *Non-Stop Hollywood* syndicated column

Los Angeles Ledger

NON-STOP HOLLYWOOD

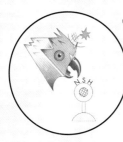

THE HOSPITAL EXPECTS LORD WILL BE SENT HOME to recuperate in about two weeks.

The broken beauty was no sooner rushed to Cedars of Lebanon yesterday when Monolithic Pictures announced "Blonde Lace" would resume shooting immediately. Other than

insisting the picture is "well on the way to completion," the studio refused to disclose any details. But a little green birdie tells me that Gene Marshall now plays a prominent role in the over-budget, over-schedule, and apparently ill-starred feature.

FOOTLOOSE SINCE HER RECENT DIVORCE from Cedric Gibbons, orchidaceous Dolores Del Rio has been seen on

INTEROFFICE MEMOS

TO: Mr. David Astor, Script Department

FROM: Mr. Lilienthal

DATE: March 29, 1941

RE: MISS GEORGIA JAMES

James works exclusively upon "Blonde Lace" until further notice. Reassign "Weak Sisters" and the Hemingway book to other writers.

TO: Miss Draper, Wardrobe Department

FROM: Mr. Lilienthal

DATE: March 29, 1941

RE: "BLONDE LACE"

Consult with production supervisor and Von Sternberg regarding revised wardrobe needs and fitting schedule. Spend as necessary. Attend to Miss Marshall's fittings yourself. Create great new image. Cool but feminine. Elegant but mysterious. Sexy but sincere. Von Sternberg will advise.

TO: Johnny Shaw, Music Department

FROM: Mr. Lilienthal

DATE: March 29, 1941

RE: "BLONDE LACE"

Consult Von Sternberg and James regarding new song, which is to be a title number sung by Miss Marshall. Something catchy to dance to. Make sure it will be a big hit. Take as much time as needed. You will audition song for me tomorrow at 8:15 a.m. in my office.

TO: Mr. Algaze, Legal Department

FROM: Mr. Lilienthal

DATE: March 29, 1941

RE: MADRA LORD

Meet me at 9 a.m. tomorrow to discuss Lord contract. Specifically review Act of God, injury, and liability clauses. Expect to accompany me to hospital later with documents.

TO: Mr. Cochran, Payroll Department

FROM: Mr. Lilienthal

DATE: March 29, 1941

RE: "BLONDE LACE"

See accompanying contracts. To confirm: Payment in full for six weeks at $5,000 per for Miss Lord. Plus a $5,000 bonus. Remit to my attention immediately. Engage Miss Marshall for new run-of-film contract at $2,500 per week plus other considerations per new memo with her counsel.

TO: Harry Hale, Publicity Department

FROM: Mr. Lilienthal

DATE: March 29, 1941

RE: "BLONDE LACE" publicity campaign

Halt speculation of "bad luck" image. Express official studio sympathy to Lord. Send newsreel crew to hospital for flower presentation. Cora Harper to do bedside broadcast at later date. Close set to all visitors. Marshall is off limits to all writers unless okayed by me personally. Expect new plot summary within 48 hours to commence formulating future exploitation campaign. Budget to come. Expected release date: July 1, 1941.

TO: Mr. Clifton Dallas, Animation Department

FROM: Mr. Lilienthal

DATE: March 29, 1941

RE: YOUR STAFF

It has come to my attention that your artists spent the entire day doing nothing but drawing cartoons of Miss Madra Lord's unfortunate accident. This must stop immediately. Confiscate and destroy.

This hasty impression of Madra Lord's downfall was given to me after our final interview by Ivy Jordan, who acquired several from the studio's cartoonists. "It's the cleanest one among them," she informed me.

—Mel

ERIK VON STERNBERG

From *Eye for Beauty*

Time—we had none.

Talent we had in abundance, with all the resources of Monolithic behind us.

A mysterious girl walks into a nightclub and finds herself entrapped in a web of white-hot glamour and frightening darkness. She unexpectedly becomes the princess of the glittering scene, but discovers death lurking in its hallways and back rooms.

A detective is taken by Marjorie's beauty. She becomes drawn to Steve's sorrow when his gallant sweetheart Vera is murdered. But they eventually begin to suspect the other one may be a killer.

The pressure builds.

Steve finds himself unable to sleep. But Marjorie strangely begins sleepwalking during the small dark hours, drifting down to the club from her penthouse above. Against her conscious will, the beautiful dreamer keeps returning to the scenes of the crimes.

There are other characters, however—a gangster, a hatcheck girl, a bandleader, a half-witted kitchen worker—and any one of them could be a murderer. Or perhaps the killer is someone else.

Let's be ambivalent about it, I told Georgia, let's arrange to make the ending as open as possible. As one, we came up with the conclusion.

There, in the dressing room mirror: "You're looking at the killer" scrawled in lipstick. A hanged person's feet reflected in the glass. And the faces of several people staring back in horror at the message.

Georgia didn't sleep for three days, fortified by club sandwiches, bourbon, and cigarettes as she slaved away, roughing out the script. She would later polish the dialogue on the set.

The great Charlie Beauchamp was yanked off another film to assist in merging the salvageable footage with our earlier tests of Gene and new scenes to be photographed under his supervision. Drawing upon the expressionist techniques I acquired during my early years with Fritz Lang at UFA and Murnau at Fox, we created an underworld of shadows that contrasted mysteriously against the bright-edged club scenes.

Fortunately, most of the new sequences we planned occurred in stark places. Corridors. Elevators. Cars. Basements. Locations that were easy and cheap to film.

Ivy Jordan

It's amazing to me how Gene accepted the incredible challenge these people proposed as if she had no other choice. Gene told me it felt like being on a roller coaster—once it started, you had to go along for the ride.

Erik worked with her like a man possessed, and possessed is exactly what he was. He would have kept Gene shooting all night long, except Rubi set down strict orders on her schedule. As it was, Gene put in twelve to fifteen hours a day in the studio between filming, rehearsing, being fitted for clothes, and doing whatever publicity things they wanted of her. Then she went home and learned her lines for the next day.

I liked Gene right away, but I'm not sure at what point she and I became close. We'd been chummy since the train and shared a lot of laughs working together on the set. By the time the accident happened, Gene seemed like the little sister I always wanted.

You know, Gene really hasn't changed so much over the years since. Oh, sure, there's that introspective side. She's always been something of a brooder.

But I don't blame her. She has every reason to be private.

While we were filming, the studio tried to shield Gene from the sharks, wolves, and other animals in the Hollywood zoo. I know for a fact they withheld from Gene tons of mail she got. Still, she couldn't help but see the magazines on the newsstands.

A lot of stuff printed about her wasn't accurate or kind. Some supposedly true accounts painted Gene as cold and aloof; a little hand puppet for Von Sternberg; a schemer who stole the picture from Madra; an icy siren who was breaking up Erik's marriage to Zena or making hot and heavy with Rubi, Trent, and half a dozen leading men of the day.

Sad but true, as much as the public and press pull for you in the beginning, there's a growing crowd out there wondering why success didn't happen to them. So they wait for you to fall on your face. It's "so you won the chariot race, well, good for you, girl, now go face the lions and see what happens."

From *Maharajah of the Movies*

The crisis exhilarated him. He always loved beating the odds.

With its new approach decided, Lilienthal personally took over as the film's producer. Makers of concurrent Monolithic features suspected that their front office decisions were actually being made by Miss Hardy, but since the results more than usually proved beneficial, few complained.

One by one over long-distance wires, Lilienthal cajoled Monolithic's New York board of directors into increasing the film's budget. One by one, he wooed exhibitors in major cities to book *Blonde Lace* as their major attraction for the Fourth of July weekend. Enormous publicity surrounding Marshall's sensational train ride made his task easier. "Everybody in the world wants to get a look at her at least once," he told them.

Before those conversations ensued, Lilienthal first met with Madra Lord at her hospital bedside. He found the injured star at the center of a three-room suite bursting with flowers; she was smoking a cigarette and flipping through a movie magazine. As he approached, she cast the magazine aside and assumed a pathetic smile.

"It hurts," she whimpered, pointing to her leg in traction. Lilienthal kissed a varnished toe nail, which protruded above the massive plaster cast, and presented Lord with a large check.

"That's for the picture's original shooting schedule and a bonus," he announced. "You've earned every penny. The studio will see to the hospital bills and you remain on salary while you recuperate. I hope that makes you feel better."

"Nobody knows the suffering I've endured," Lord replied. "I should sue."

"Be my guest," Lilienthal shrugged. "That was a mighty peculiar accident. I'd be just as interested as you in whatever the investigators might turn up." There was a long pause as mogul and movie star contemplated one another. "Listen, Madra, I like to think that the worst is behind us. So let's look forward to your next picture."

"No, I'd rather talk about this one. How do you intend to finish it without me?"

"We've come up with a new twist."

"Oh, yes? Let's hear it."

Lilienthal dismissed the hovering nurses with a curt "scram."

Waiting outside, various studio lawyers, Lord's agent, and Erik von Sternberg were eventually summoned to Lord's bedside while the hospital staff loitered curiously in the hall. Occasionally, Lord's voice, shrill with anger, pierced through the closed door.

BENNY MAJORS

No, that was not a pleasant afternoon. Not by a long shot. The lawyers kept invoking this clause and that one in the contracts. Madra was writhing around like a den of snakes were in bed with her. And from the way Lilienthal steamed, you could have cooked breakfast on his head. Me, I kept my yap shut unless I was spoken to.

The upshot was that Madra didn't cozy up to the new story one bit, but there wasn't anything she could do to prevent the studio from finishing it their way.

At first, she refused to have anything to do with the retakes that Erik wanted her to make once she could film again. He got all Viennese schmaltzy with her, explaining the retakes needed to match the new scenario. But when Madra kept balking, Erik went all icy and said that if he were forced to, he'd employ a double. He only hoped she recalled how terrible *Saratoga* looked when they used Harlow's stand-in to finish the picture after she passed away.

The hardest point involved a new scene showing Vera's murder. Madra said she was superstitious about it; that she had never died in a picture before and thought it was bad luck. "It hasn't harmed Garbo's career and she dies all the time," said Erik, again threatening to use a double. "I can just as easily shoot you from the back as from the front."

Then Lilienthal reminded Madra how her seven-year contract with Monolithic would expire in 1942. "Have you given any thought where you'd like to go after you leave us?" He knew full well how no other studio would put up with her whims like they did. Madra knew it, too. But she simply blew a ring of smoke at him and said, "More than you know."

Finally, Lilienthal said that if she'd cooperate, he'd let Madra make *Mrs. Grant* as her next feature. It had long been one of her dreams, but the studio believed that after *Gone With the Wind*, the public wouldn't want another Civil War picture for years to come. "Probably we've got a war coming now," said Lilienthal. "Maybe it would be a good idea to show a lady who helps her man battle his way to the top." Thrilled, Madra started gabbing about maybe getting Spencer Tracy or Joel McCrea to play General Grant.

Lilienthal rose and said, "We've got a deal then? You'll help us finish *Blonde Lace*?"

Madra flashed a big smile. "Of course, darling. Just as soon as I'm able. Every last inch of it."

CORA HARPER
From *Non-Stop Hollywood* syndicated column

Los Angeles Ledger

NON-STOP HOLLYWOOD

SOMETIMES IT TAKES A BAD BREAK TO SHOW A STAR'S TRUE COLORS, and Madra Lord's gallant quest to help Monolithic complete "Blonde Lace" is a lesson to the industry. Still prone upon her hospital bed, she has selflessly agreed to act in new scenes that can be filmed while she is sitting down. Doctors predict that she will be able to resume work in four weeks or so.

ELLIE DRAPER
From *Designers on Design*

At first we hoped that we could simply refit Gene with some of Madra's wardrobe. But the character Gene played didn't suit those modes, and besides, what might look fine on Madra did not correspond with Gene's style. Their figures, color, and natural flair were too dissimilar.

Although *Blonde Lace* was made in black and white, Erik demanded specific costume colors. Typical Middle-European arrogance—and from a man yet!—but, fortunately, Erik's choices almost invariably were correct. The chartreuse of the flower girl frock registered beautifully on film. The silvery nightdress Gene wore added to the shimmering impression she made in those sleepwalking scenes.

Gene was sportier in casual life, of course. Heavens, she was still a girl: Gene turned eighteen in the middle of filming. I remember it because the seamstresses brought a little cake into the fitting room. Later, I heard that everyone from the grips on the set to the mail room girls gave her cake that day. The poor thing must have blown out a million candles all over the studio.

GEORGIA JAMES
From *Hollywood Talks*

Oh, I was nuts about that tune from the start. "I love blonde lace, and a charming face, and a place where anything can happen when we dance . . . ."

That Johnny Shaw really knew how to write a song, didn't he? It was on the Hit Parade for months on end. Folks have never stopped humming it.

Since Madra's "You Floor Me" was such a gaudy affair, we thought it a good idea to ease this number into the film—use it during an after-hours rehearsal—the club deserted, with a spooky twilight about it, and Gene in that black tuxedo, dancing in a spotlight. "And who knows what might be watching her in the shadows?" said Erik, with that possum smile of his.

Johnny was such a swell performer on his own that we pegged him as her piano player in the scene. We figured he'd know best how to make Gene look like a pro. Turns out she didn't need help. Johnny had been around for a while—big bands and radio before he came to Mono—and he was dumbfounded at how quick Gene was on the pickup. "Only Garland and Crosby work faster," he told me. The dance director said much the same about teaching her the routine.

She sure looked dreamy doing it on-screen. Maybe, said Lilienthal in the projection room, we should start thinking next about a musical for Gene.

Me, I didn't need to think about anything but getting *Blonde Lace* finished. Erik was shooting one scene while I was banging out the next.

HARRY HALE
From ASF's Oral History Project

We had to hire extra help to answer Gene's fan mail. The press ate up every photo and release we put out and demanded more. Because we kept such a tight lid on her personal publicity, some of the junk they invented was outrageous. She was a

debutante. She was a child of the slums. She was a home-wrecker. She was a runaway bride.

Finally the day came when the Hearst chain of newspapers and several big magazines said they were sick of running our canned stuff and wanted to get their own, or else they would not cooperate with the campaign for *Blonde Lace* we were developing. So we agreed to send Gene out for some nights on the town where the photographers and reporters could get to her a bit.

It was all carefully arranged. Once Gene was done shooting for the day, she'd go back to her bungalow and get dolled up in whatever glamour getups the wardrobe department thought best. We got a couple of Hollywood's leading bachelors to squire her to the local hot spots. Trent Osborn was in-between flames at the moment and since putting them together would be great publicity for the picture, they went out at least twice a week for the duration of the filming.

TRENT OSBORN
From *My Bed of Roses*

For years afterward, stories circulated about my torrid "romance" with Gene. Nothing to it, I'm sorry to say. All manufactured by the studio and the fertile minds of the press. We might have looked lovey-dovey in public, but it was strictly for-show business.

Still, Gene was fascinated by finally seeing for herself every famous place and every movie star she'd heard about all her life, and I was just the guy to show her. The Mocambo was the hot new joint. Ciro's, Romanoff's, and Earl Carroll's place were among my haunts. Old-time Hollywood late in its heyday. The whole town was charged up, electric.

So after work and on RL's dime, out we'd go. I had a sharp Lincoln roadster, which I'd drive off the lot with Gene next to me and a studio car full of press agents following. Me in black-tie, sometimes white-tie, depending on where we went. Gene always in some incredible gown.

Outside, say, The Cocoanut Grove, the press would grab pictures as we signed autographs and walked in. Next, we'd make our big entrance, cameras flashing from behind every palm tree. Then we'd get settled at a table. More pictures. Then we'd dance. Again with the flashbulbs. Finally, the photographers were sent away and we could settle in.

Gene would have one glass of champagne and no more. Then we'd talk as I polished off the magnum. Mostly about the picture, of course. A couple of press agents were at the next table. Gene's bodyguard, Slapsie, would go off to shoot craps behind the coatroom. Everybody else in the place tried not to look too often or long at us. Back in those days, the public was far more respectful of celebrities and usually kept their distance.

Still, it was easier to frequent the spots where the stars gathered. Somehow you'd have more privacy when a lot of the people there were just as famous as you. When the likes of Lana, Jimmy, Claudette, Norma, Errol, and more of that kind are all in one room, Trent and Gene don't look so conspicuous at their table.

Once or twice, I got deep into my cups and told Gene about the females in my life. Somehow I felt that I could trust her. By the way, let me state right here that the reason no one's ever dug up any dirt about Gene Marshall over the years is the fact that there isn't any.

We'd last about an hour. Remember, we'd been up since four in the morning, so by ten o'clock at night, we were having trouble keeping our eyes open. Most times, Slapsie would take Gene home. She usually fell asleep on the way.

Once Gene asked me if I'd drive her out to Pasadena and then get lost. As a favor to her. There was someone special she wanted to see. Sure, I said. We got to Ciro's early, did our bit for the camera, and left. On the way, we stopped at a gas station where Gene changed into casual clothes. What a girl next door might wear going to the movies. Which is what Gene said she'd be doing with a fellow named Paul Ames. He'd bring her home afterward.

MARSHA HUNT
From a letter to Mel Odom (November 11, 1999)
Gene Marshall? Yes, I did meet her, but only fleetingly at large functions—except for one occasion when we lunched together, and that was by chance. It would have been around 1941—yes, that's right. I was doing a picture at Monolithic on loan from MGM.

We arrived at the studio commissary at the same time, each alone, and were waiting to be seated. The hostess beckoned and we both started forward, stopped short deferring to the other, laughed, and decided to share the table.

I found her endearing, composed, and poised for one so young. Still, she struck me as faintly wistful and maybe vulnerable. The lovely pale blue eyes seemed to hold a hint of sadness. I recall what a pleasure it was to gaze into those remarkable eyes. The only eyes I recall finding so spellbinding belonged to a little girl. I used to choose a seat in the MGM commissary that would face in her direction in preference even to the long central writers' table. Habitually, there sat Gable, Tracy, Taylor, Eddy, Stewart, Pidgeon, Powell, Young, Heflin. They had discovered the wit level to be enjoyed in the company of writers and peals of robust laughter would roll out from that table. But as great as that view was the pleasure of watching a very young Elizabeth Taylor, then shooting *National Velvet*. And that's a good word for her eyes—velvet.

But back to Gene. I can't tell you much about our lunch talk—it was half a century ago! But I remember how intently she listened to my responses to her questions about being a film actress. I was already a veteran of twenty-five or so motion pictures, a seasoned old gal of twenty-three.

We discovered much in common, about our beginnings at least. Each of us came from the northeast coast and had happy childhoods with ideal parents in comfortable but not rich circumstances. Each fixed on goals in screen acting early in life, taking part in childhood plays at every chance, seeing every movie we could, doing some fashion modeling—but no cheesecake or swimsuit jobs. Each began in films at major studios at age seventeen amid much hoopla, although hers was a hundred times mine. And each was so wholesomely raised that we kept our heads despite the hoopla, intent on learning and improving our craft, not focused on the glitz and glitter.

I'm afraid I can't quote you a single word she said. She almost never commented, just asked questions. Thoughtful and reserved, she had an aura of mystery about her—a quality usually associated with inscrutable, mature glamour queens such as Garbo and Dietrich. But here was a fresh, unspoiled girl in her teens who prompted the same curiosity.

And because, though sweet and cordial, she revealed so little of her inner self and vouchsafed so little verbally, one couldn't estimate her intelligence. Was this breathtaking beauty catapulted into the national spotlight by her gorgeousness alone, a deeply wise and careful strategist of her life and career, employing intellect as well as instinct in her acting performances? Or was she a simple soul, uncluttered by complexities or much cerebration, pliable and therefore responsive to direction and able to provide whatever was coached or asked for?

We may never know. And all these years later it's part of why we still remain fascinated by the sweet dreaminess of Gene Marshall.

ERIK VON STERNBERG
From *Eye for Beauty*

Exhilaration and exhaustion consumed me.

March melted into April. I did not see my new son Christopher until three days after his birth because I was so absorbed with the film. Zena understood, thank God, and gave me her blessing to construct my latest cathedral without having to worry about family concerns. They would be there, safe and sound, whenever I was able to stagger home from the studio.

Looking back upon making the film, I only recall fevered flashes. How we achieved the claustrophobic terror of the elevator sequence. Walking Gene endlessly up and down the grand staircase, preparing her for the recognition scene. Finding the correct angle for the discovery in the boiler room. Watching Gene's completed song and dance routine dazzle everyone. That magical afternoon when we completed the mirror scene in a single continuous take.

I could have gone on making *Blonde Lace* forever.

ALICE MARSHALL
From a letter to Dr. Marshall

I haven't told Katie yet, but I plan to come home, perhaps as early as next week. I have nothing to do here and it's silly for me to sit around while Katie makes this movie. I can't help the child with her acting, can I?

From all that I see, she'll be taken care of. Goodness, the studio gives her a bodyguard, a maid, and nice people to take her anywhere she needs to go. Besides, Allie, Katie never gave us a bit of worry in New York so there's no reason to expect she will be any different here.

Anyway, Ned lives close by, and Katie has made wonderful new friends. This Ivy is a smart girl who's lived in Hollywood all her life, and I know that she'll do anything for Katie. Our girl will be perfectly fine for however long it takes for them to finish this picture, then she'll come home to us for a while.

But I don't think we should expect to keep Katie long. She loves what she's doing and from the looks of it, she's very good. (And why shouldn't she be?) They showed me parts of the movie in a little theater they have at the studio. It's the strangest thing to see her on the screen. After a while I forgot that it was Katie until I saw her kissing Trent Osborn, which was confusing, because he wasn't acting at all like he does when he's not acting, if you understand what I mean.

Anyway, it looks to me like Katie is just as good as somebody like Sylvia Sidney. So of course they will want her to make more movies and that means she will have to live out here. We need to face it—Katie belongs here. She may as well learn right away how to make a life for herself without you or me getting in her way.

From *Maharajah of the Movies*

True to her word, Lord appeared once again on the set of *Blonde Lace* a month later. Everything was planned so the actress could work mostly in close-up. Already absorbed in preproduction details for *Mrs. Grant*, Lord showed no interest in firing up further feuding with Marshall. Believing, she admitted later, that *Blonde Lace* was marred beyond all hope by its revisions, Lord decided to make the best of a bad job and filmed her scenes with brisk expertise.

After one exchange, Lord went so far as to compliment Marshall's performance. "You're pretty good for a beginner."

Lord was too immersed in her next picture to bother viewing any rushes as *Blonde Lace* was quickly cut and assembled, nor did she attend the sneak previews in Santa Barbara and Long Beach.

Lilienthal drove out to the first preview with Miss Hardy, dictating memos along the way. Von Sternberg and his staff met him at the Alhambra in Santa Barbara. Supporting player Ivy Jordan was there, but none of its other stars. Marshall said she wasn't ready to see herself on the screen yet, and Osborn had just eloped with a Pasadena heiress he'd met only weeks earlier.

As *Blonde Lace* unwound, producer and director stood at the rear of the auditorium, judging the spectators' reaction. The Santa Barbara audience was considered a "sophisticated" group by the industry, equivalent to Manhattan viewers. A murmur arose as the title and Gene Marshall's name glowed across the screen, followed by the sight of her stepping off a streetcar and advancing toward the camera through a drizzle of rain, blonde hair shining in the black-and-white gloom.

Profound silence, broken only by appreciative laughter during the comedy scenes, indicated that viewers were immersed in this tale of a beautiful sleepwalker. The unexpected murder of Madra Lord's character jolted them into screams, followed by apparently even deeper absorption as the story strangely descended into darkness and played itself out. As the final image faded into "The End," a storm of applause erupted.

The preview cards passed out among the audience came back wildly positive. All were extremely enthusiastic regarding Marshall while Lord received some of her best comments in several pictures. "So far not so bad," said Lilienthal. "Now let's see how it goes over with the Farm Belt crowd."

The next night in Long Beach, a rowdy audience cheered Lord's murder and let loose with admiring whistles as Marshall went into her dance. Afterward, applause was lusty and once again the cards came up mostly aces. Tightening was called for, and the exposition needed clarifying, but it was obvious that the picture represented a major achievement.

"Christmas comes earlier than usual this year," said Lilienthal jubilantly, endorsing Von Sternberg's plans to polish the film. He immediately began negotiations with Marshall's advisers for a long-term contract. As postproduction work rapidly went forward, news of the film's sensational reaction spread across the industry. Banks holding mortgages on Monolithic agreed to forgo demanding further payments until after *Blonde Lace* opened in July.

When Von Sternberg uneasily approached Lord about reshooting a moment of the crucial scene in which she had earlier met her accident, the star was surprisingly amenable. "I hear the picture is perfect already," she laughed. "But if you really need that bit redone, Erik, I'm ready whenever you are."

GEORGIA JAMES

From *Hollywood Talks*

Honestly, no one was more surprised than me to see how swell *Blonde Lace* grew on people. I was so chained to the process that I couldn't gauge the film clearly until I finally saw it with a real movie audience. I was thrilled to watch people go nuts over something so offbeat. Erik and Lilienthal were busting with excitement.

Gene's impact was tremendous. You could feel the people sitting around you fall in love with her. Later, Erik had to go back and edit in a few extra seconds to her very first close-up just to allow for the a-a-h of pleasure everyone felt as Gene's face filled the screen. Trent was a pip, too, and so was Ivy in a turnaround role for her. As for Madra, well, she was living proof that less was more.

Lilienthal called me in during postproduction. Manuscripts and books were stacked high on his desk. He told me to go over them with an eye toward future Gene Marshall films. The one on top was *Kept in the Dark* and still tagged "Best." Lilienthal looked at me and smiled.

IVY JORDAN

You know, I had no idea that I was a halfway decent dramatic actress until I saw myself in *Blonde Lace.* Or that Madra was anything more than a four-handkerchief ham bone. And who knew whether Gene could act at all? I mean, you couldn't tell on the set, except she was easy to work with.

Those first audiences went mad for the picture, and especially for Gene. She didn't go to the sneak preview—said she'd take our word for however it went—but there was no way Mom Marshall wasn't going to see how her baby went over with a movie audience. She delayed going east just long enough to come with me to Santa Barbara. The Ames family was on hand, too. Mom Marshall cried during the entire picture and practically all the way home.

Let me see, that must have been about a week or so before our other little calamity.

From *Maharajah of the Movies*

By the third week in May, Lilienthal was coordinating the elaborate exhibition campaign for the July release of *Blonde Lace* even as Von Sternberg supervised its final touches.

Late on the morning of May 22, the director was slated to complete his last bit of filming: a retake of a pivotal scene between Gene Marshall and Madra Lord on the nightclub set.

Miss Hardy's appointment book for Lilienthal that same day included a 2 P.M. meeting regarding details for the New York premiere of *Blonde Lace* at the Regency. At 4:30 P.M., Marshall was scheduled to affix her name to an exclusive three-year, ten-picture contract with the studio—while being filmed by Monolithic's newsreel cameras.

But the meeting would not happen. The contract went unsigned. The afternoon had scarcely begun when Lilienthal found himself quite literally fighting to save his studio from total destruction.

Shock

Cora Harper

From Luncheon with the Stars radio broadcast (May 22, 1941)

It's high noon and high time for Luncheon with the Stars
here at the Green Parrot with your trusty guide to Hollywood's heavens, Cora Harper.

  I'm breaking bread with MGM's singing lovebirds,
Jeanette MacDonald and Nelson Eddy, who are just completing "I Married an Angel." So let's dish! For our first
course, kids, I want to hear exactly how you two—
Oh, my!—I'm afraid there's a little bit of an earthquake going on! Heavens, might this be a reminder of your success in "San Francisco," Jeanette?
Oh dear, it's getting worse—you know, we'd best get up and go somewhere
until it—oh, dear—yes, let's all follow Nelson. Hurry!

Madra Lord

From Dark Radiance

There I was, positioned once again on those fatal checkerboard tiles at Stage Four.
The camera was rolling, Eric intently poised on the other side. I was confronting
Gene Marshall. "But that means you're my baby sister—"

  And suddenly I felt the floor beneath me move!

Horror chilled me. I nearly swooned with déjà vu. Then in the next instant I realized, almost with relief, that we were in the midst of an earthquake.

Erik von Sternberg
From *Eye for Beauty*

For a moment, I feared it was the end of the world.

As the soundstage plunged into chaotic darkness, the final image that indelibly burned into my retina was the sight of a panicked Madra being dragged by Gene across the undulating floor like a well-dressed sack of turnips. The din of crashing objects and splintering wood rose to a horrifying crescendo and subsided. The quake was over as suddenly as it began.

Amid the blackness, a babble of frightened voices swelled like a tide of fear. Did no one among the crew have a flashlight?

From *Maharajah of the Movies*

Registering 5.9 on the Richter scale, the relatively moderate Izquierdo earthquake was limited to the western Los Angeles environs, but caused considerable damage to flimsy construction close to the fault line. Practically all of the Monolithic complex remained intact despite its shaking.

Surveying his kingdom through the splintered picture windows of his office, Lilienthal saw few signs of serious harm. Aside from cracks and a few dislodged bricks, his dozen soundstages stood intact. A water main had broken, spewing a muddy geyser into the air. Studio workers rushed among the maze of alleys. He spied most of his executives clustered below in the garden, excitedly talking.

"What are you clowns doing?" he shouted at them. "Get out and see what's wrong!" As they scattered, Lilienthal turned to Miss Hardy, her memo book poised. "Let's first see whether anyone is hurt," he began, and then broke off, staring beyond the roof of Stage Four.

Inky columns of smoke were vigorously spiraling up in the distance.

He immediately knew what was happening. "Call the fire department," he barked. "We've got trouble at the film lab." Telephone lines were dead, reported Miss Hardy. As Lilienthal raced out the door, he grimly chuckled, "So now we'll find out how good our own fire system works."

The cluster of frowsy frame structures housing the editing rooms and film laboratory had been wracked by the quake. As staircases collapsed and ceilings fell into the workrooms, the volatile nitrate film stock exploded into flames in half a dozen areas. Within a few minutes, the tottering buildings were bonfires. A lazy breeze fanned the fire toward the soundstages.

By the time Lilienthal reached the scene, paint was already blistering the facade of nearby Stage Six. The studio fire engine roared up. The squadron chief told him they had scant water pressure because of underground ruptures in the mains.

IVY JORDAN

Oh, it was going to be a red-letter day, you know. Gene was going to formally sign the million-dollar contract that old man Ames had hammered out with the studio.

As luck would have it, we were filming retakes of the big Marjorie-Vera scene. Its dialogue had been rewritten to match the new story. Gene was in her flower girl costume. Erik was shooting them from a head-and-shoulders angle so you couldn't see the crutch Madra still leaned upon. I was in the background again in extremely soft-focus.

The quake rolled in from a distance. Madra screamed and grabbed for Gene. Erik's chair collapsed beneath him. The shaking grew worse. I ducked into the frame of the checkroom door just as all hell rained down. Unbelievable noise. Then the lights went out.

After the quake died away, everyone began babbling as if to make sure they're still alive. I kept saying, "What a doozie!" It was black as pitch in there—no windows, you know—and no one could see a thing.

Then somebody finally managed to open one of the sliding doors at the far end of the stage. A big bright square of sunlight appeared with blue sky beyond.

Some people ran for it, scared about aftershocks. Utter confusion. Dust choking the air. Sets collapsed and junk strewn all over the floor. I spied Erik crouching a few feet away, tending to poor Charlie, who'd been beaned on the head by a lighting pole.

Gene sat under a table, rocking Madra back and forth, trying to calm her down. Royal pain that Madra was, you still couldn't help but feel a pang for her. She was

Opposite Page: Ivy Jordan

152

jelly, quivering with terror. "The floor, the floor," she kept moaning. Gene held on to her real tight.

Suddenly Madra snapped back together. She shook her head a couple of times and you could almost hear a click, as if a door were being shut somewhere inside. She pushed Gene away and crawled from beneath the table. "I'm all right now," she said as Gene and I helped her to a chair. "Anybody got a smoke?"

TRENT OSBORN

From *My Bed of Roses*

The quake hit when a lot of us were in the commissary. Tables rocked and dishes broke, but few people seemed to panic. There was even a scattering of applause when the shaking stopped.

"God just dropped one mighty heavy hairpin," cracked Georgia.

Time for a pick-me-up, I thought, and liberated a bottle of bonded bourbon from the bar, which had spilled most of its contents. After toasting our survival a few times, we went outside and spotted thick clouds of smoke mushrooming over the far end of the lot.

When we got there, it was obvious that the editing rooms were beyond saving. Practically every window was roaring with flames. RL was in the middle of a cluster of people, snapping out orders. Our fire truck crew was desperately trying to hook up directly into the cistern beneath the water tower.

But before they could tap into it, we could see the roof on the stage next door begin smoking like the devil, and people started lugging cameras and furniture out. Ellie Draper tore through the door, pushing a rack of Victorian ball gowns, stopping only to swipe away at sparks landing on the costumes.

Vans and cars appeared from nowhere, and folks began dragging items away from other places near to the fire. The makeup building and publicity offices seemed most in jeopardy. Ted Westland and his crew were hurling wigs down from a second-story window into a pickup truck. In the middle of it, a couple of our own newsreel boys materialized out of the smoke and began filming everything in sight.

That was the crazy thing: It all looked like a scene from a picture. The final reel of *The Last Days of Pompeii* done in modern clothes. Except that actors dressed like cowboys and harem girls and Transylvania peasants were mixed up among everybody else.

Every so often, a strong breeze would make the flames shoot higher. Everybody was worried that if the wind kept up and they couldn't control the fire, the whole studio might burn. Monolithic was mostly a bunch of buildings packed closely together—stages, administration offices, workshops, warehouses—stuffed with everything flammable under the sun. It was a sixty-acre tinderbox.

Suddenly, marching through the smoke came a line of wildly excited kid actors from the studio schoolhouse right down the street. Helping their teacher take them somewhere safer on the lot was Gene, who'd managed to get all five Bratzanjammer Boys firmly in tow.

Nearby, a makeshift bucket brigade was scooping water pooled around a broken hydrant and was wetting down buildings closest to the fire. Along with buckets, they were using pots taken from the commissary, trash cans—even a couple of medieval helmets from god knows what movie—to wet down the neighboring buildings. Maybe two hundred people were lined up in a chain, passing their containers along the street. Johnny Shaw, Ivy, and others we knew were on the line, so Georgia and I joined them.

Everyone scattered for a second as Madra's open Cadillac came zooming around the corner and screeched to a stop in front of the publicity office. Madra's maid and chauffeur tore out of the car, with Madra limping after them on crutches. I ran over and asked what they were doing. Madra said that she'd be damned if every portrait and still taken during her career was going to go up in smoke with the publicity building.

HARRY HALE
From ASF's Oral History Project

I was actually off the lot when the earthquake happened, bringing Dame Elinor Pomeroy back to the studio after a morning tea held in her honor at the Hollywood Cricket Club. We scarcely felt the quake ourselves, since we were in a moving car. But the damage appeared more obvious the nearer we got to Monolithic. When we arrived, we couldn't drive our way on to the lot because of all the cars and trucks and people coming out through the front gates.

Dame Elinor, who'd actually gotten her title for doing Red Cross work during World War I, scurried off to the infirmary to help. I made my way toward the fire, which looked worse every second. Stage Six was a furnace. Inside, we'd been shooting *Major Pendennis,* and the place was crammed with 1840s London interiors and furniture, all of it burning.

Across the way, John Barrymore sat upon a throne someone had dragged out, watching the blazing stage with a quizzical smile on his face. He saluted me with a highball as I raced past. Happy Trales rode herd on a pack of horses heading for the back gate, yipping like a teenager. I spied Cliff Davis and his lunatic bunch perched in the windows of the animation building, each of them holding siphon bottles of seltzer.

I never saw the boss look so much like a Roman general. In his wet shirtsleeves, covered with soot, he marched around giving his orders. I remember that when I reached Lilienthal, he was turning away from the fire chief to tell the newsreel men they should step back to grab a wider angle. Then he saw me. "You better get to your office and save what you can," he yelled. "We don't have any water to waste there." He was going to protect the stages and warehouses first and worry about the rest later.

The publicity building was already ablaze when I reached it. People were hauling boxes and files out. I wanted to grab a few personal items from my office, but couldn't get up the stairs for the heat and smoke.

From *Maharajah of the Movies*

When the roof collapsed into the Stage Six inferno, a fiery cloud of flaming cinders and sparks rained down across the lot. Blazes igniting upon the Stage Four and Stage Five roofs were stamped out before they could cause significant damage. Contained within its half-crumbled concrete walls, the Stage Six inferno continued to burn itself out ferociously, but the fire's western march toward the downwind row of stages was effectively halted.

Girl Star

Scanning the scene from atop Stage Five, a weary but jubilant Lilienthal observed the Los Angeles Fire Department arrive to hose down his endangered warehouses opposite the fire. At its furthest perimeter, the facade of the wood-shingled animation department was scorched black, yet had miraculously withstood

the flames. Makeup and the publicity offices had been reduced to glowing mounds. Most adjacent structures had been rescued by the bucket brigades' frenzied efforts. At the heart of the devastation, only smoking pits indicated where the editing buildings once stood.

Lilienthal looked at his watch and noted that scarcely an hour had elapsed since the quake struck. Turning to Miss Hardy, who stood at his side with every steel-gray hair in place, he inquired whether the studio's insurance premiums were in order. Assured that they were, he violently hugged her and they rapidly toured the lot to assess the damage.

There were no deaths and few serious injuries, reported Dame Elinor Pomeroy, who had taken over the infirmary's operation. The worst cases had been taken to hospitals while others with bruises and bumped heads were resting under her supervision.

An ashen Erik von Sternberg appeared. Placing his hand on Lilienthal's shoulder, he quietly informed the mogul that all of the footage of *Blonde Lace* had been destroyed in the fire. Then Von Sternberg sank to his knees and wept.

Erik von Sternberg

From *Eye for Beauty*

Who knows what I did that apocalyptic afternoon?

The stories of the fire are so apocryphal that I am credited with a dozen simultaneous deeds in a dozen places. It's true that I initially helped Charlie Beauchamp reach the infirmary, but I cannot account for my actions after I returned to the fire and realized that every vestige of *Blonde Lace* was being consumed along with the editing department.

I went temporarily mad with grief.

The night before we had sneaked the film again. That morning, Vicky Steiner was scheduled to edit an assortment of my last changes and insertions into the final cut. We were virtually finished; the Marjorie-Vera exchange I was shooting at the moment of the quake was to be the last piece of the intricate puzzle. We were only a few days away from striking the final release prints. As far as I knew, every inch of our various work prints, negatives, and alternate footage had been removed from the vault and was in Vicky's possession in the editing rooms.

So my stomach turned with horror at the sight of the hideously tumbled and blazing structure. One of the editors told me that most of the staff had been in the commissary when the quake struck, or certainly someone would have been killed when the building was all but wrenched apart. Vicky had been pulled unconscious from the wreckage and taken elsewhere.

Had anything inside been rescued, I wondered? The editor didn't believe so, since the place burst into flames almost instantly. Whatever was in there was gone, he reckoned. *Blonde Lace* was all laid out there on the editing tables when they broke for lunch, he remembered. That was when I went haywire.

The next several hours passed in a hazy swirl. Perhaps I did try to throw myself into the inferno, as some have reported. Maybe I truly did share a bottle of Veuve Cliquot with Jack Barrymore. I know that later I made my way home to find Zena and the children safe. But before that, I have a terrible recollection of Reuben Lilienthal's soot-streaked face going white when I told him the news.

There was one other person who had to learn, directly from my lips, of the cremation of all our dreams. So I desperately searched for Gene. I found her at last on the Home Town set, watching some of the child actors play. It was the best place to keep them safe until the confusion died down, she said.

Gene straightaway asked me if the rumors she'd heard about the film's loss were true. When I nodded yes, Gene's blue eyes flooded. But I think it was more with sorrow for my loss than with any thought for herself.

Then she walked the children over to the commissary to get them something to eat.

GEORGIA JAMES
From *Hollywood Talks*
My hands bleeding from the bucket brigade, I spotted Madra as she drove off like the Queen of Sheba, her convertible overflowing with stuff grabbed from the publicity building. She never once glanced back.

Aftershock

CORA HARPER

From *Non-Stop Hollywood* syndicated column

Los Angeles Ledger

NON-STOP HOLLYWOOD

CERTAINLY THE MOST SHOCKING ASPECT of this cataclysmic event is the total destruction of "Blonde Lace" in the terrific blaze that nearly engulfed Monolithic Pictures yesterday. "Major Pendennis" was only a week into production, but "Blonde Lace" was virtually complete when disaster struck the studio.

"I can replace soundstages and film labs," mourns Reuben Lilienthal. "But there is no way on earth we can remake this picture. We are heartbroken over the loss of this major motion picture."

The sight of Erik von Sternberg hysterically sifting through the smoking ashes of the editing labs was one of the most affecting among many scenes of tragedy upon the lot. He is resting in seclusion today, tended by his wife, silent screen legend Zena Thor.

The loss of the picture is a particularly hard blow for the studio, which spent a fortune on its making. Hopes were high that "Blonde Lace," said to be a sensational new kind of film by those who witnessed its sneak previews, would replenish the empty Monolithic coffers while launching the screen career of Gene Marshall. Now the film is gone, and so is Miss Marshall's introduction to moviegoers.

ALSO IN QUAKE NEWS, Deanna Durbin was forced to cut short her honeymoon with Vaughn Paul to rush back to Universal to reshoot the entire

From *Maharajah of the Movies*

Monolithic was reeling. As an improvised makeup department was assembled on a vacant soundstage, damage costs mounted. Before Tuesday afternoon was over, Lilienthal realized he did not have funds to make immediate repairs and maintain payroll. Insurance claims would not be settled for a time, and salaries and weekly operating costs had to be met.

The studio's credit seriously overextended, Lilienthal's attempts to borrow met with a chill response. Perhaps, said several bankers, a more fiscally responsible executive leadership was required. After an emergency session, Monolithic's New York board of directors announced that a management review team would arrive Friday afternoon.

Casting his eyes about his luxurious office, Lilienthal cursed the day when he chose to construct his administration building instead of new editing labs.

Outside arrangements to process current films would be exorbitant. The cost of replacing smashed equipment all over the studio was appalling. "Buying the new hair dryers alone will bankrupt us," groaned Lilienthal.

Every film under way on the lot had suffered damage, but most would be able to resume shooting in a few days. The incinerated sets and period costumes for *Major Pendennis* were a serious loss, but scarcely the magnitude of the *Blonde Lace* disaster.

Its insurance canceled in the wake of Lord's accident, the film's loss represented over a million dollars. Lilienthal had scarcely realized how much *Blonde Lace* meant to the studio's fortunes until it had vanished. The film was slated as the studio's major summer release, and nothing could be substituted. Beyond that, his miserable awareness that *Blonde Lace* was a destroyed masterpiece was too painful for him to contemplate for long.

"Money, money, money," he muttered between phone calls. *Deep Devotion* had done well in New York and other big cities, but had flopped miserably in the hinterlands. Other recent Monolithic features in release hadn't proved very profitable. He instructed his bank to transfer any remaining personal assets into the studio's accounts. His home was already mortgaged. Lilienthal had even borrowed from his two ex-wives.

The *Blonde Lace* contingent was in a sorry state. Von Sternberg was taken home and sedated. Marshall had gone back to her hotel quarters to find its ceiling had fallen in. Osborn was reported on a drinking spree. Only Lord dropped by to commiserate with Lilienthal over *Blonde Lace,* the last in the procession of employees to see him that long day.

Sympathetic as she was over Lilienthal's predicament, Lord could not help but express her opinion of the cause of his woes. "That Marshall girl is a jinx," she said. "We've had nothing but trouble ever since she got here."

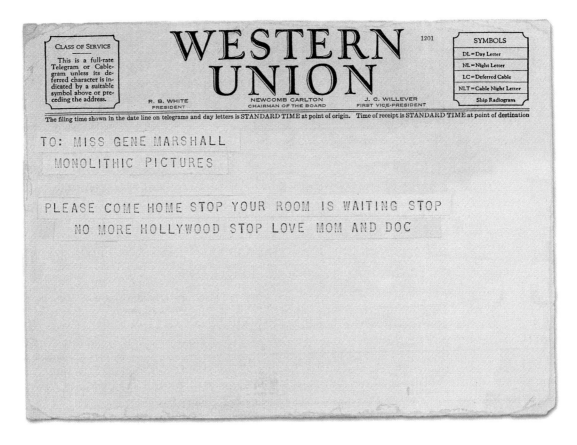

IVY JORDAN

I lost a few tiles off the roof and a breakfront of Chinese plates, but my house was fine otherwise. I was glad to give Gene a place to stay after she discovered that her hotel bungalow had been wrecked. We were able to rescue most of her things and put them in the guest room.

We sat up most of that night, talking. Gene was completely in shock over *Blonde Lace*. I wasn't any better. Million-dollar movies don't just disappear in a bonfire, you know. Though I can think of lots of pictures that might've been better off had someone put a match to them.

But to lose something like *Blonde Lace*! Devastating. Me, I knew that I could roll with the punches. I'd been through worse quakes. I'd done films before and would doubtless do more. But *Blonde Lace* was Gene's very first movie. For the last couple of months, she had let it consume every living inch of herself. Every minute of her life had gone into that movie. And now it was gone. And she hadn't even seen the darned thing!

Her parents were wild for her to return on the next train out.

Gene wasn't sure what she was going to do. And she worried whether she'd been bad luck for everybody. Well, I told her that was nonsense, but secretly I knew she had a point.

Around two o'clock in the morning, there was a pounding at the front door. In rushed Paul Ames, all worked up. He asked to see Gene. Alone. I got lost for a while; when I came back, Paul had gone. Gene was curled up in a chair with a mystified look on her face.

Paul had proposed to her. Out of the blue. He'd been upset at the thought that Gene might have been harmed and suddenly realized he loved her.

So, I said, you could do a lot worse than Paul. He's a genuine catch. Looks, smarts, loads of money, and he certainly appeared to be a sweet guy.

Gene laughed a little. She scarcely knew him. She had thanked Paul, but told him it wasn't the time to think of such things.

Well, I said, your very first earthquake and your very first proposal. Quite a day.

Gene gave me a mischievous look. How did I know it was her *first* proposal?

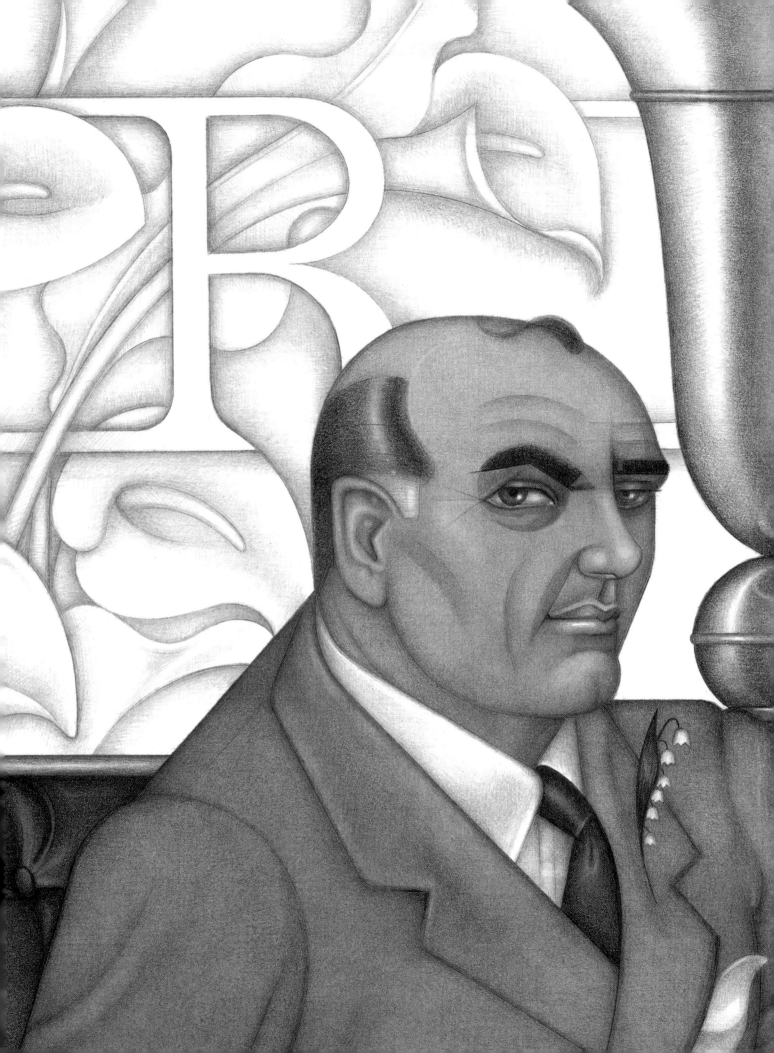

MADRA LORD

From *Dark Radiance*

I was a fool. It was madness. I should have known better.

That terrible afternoon, as I sat in my car and watched Reuben battle that fire, my heart melted at the raw power he radiated. Dirty, raging, unconquerable, Reuben saved that entire studio from the flames with his bare hands and his iron will. A real man among the jackals of Hollywood.

I recalled that sweet time half a dozen years earlier, when he and I had first encountered each other. When Reuben wooed me to join him at Monolithic. If we had not embarked upon a professional relationship, I felt sure we would have had some other kind of a union.

Perhaps it was not too late.

At home, I was thankful to discover little damage. A few broken treasures. Had I stayed at home that night, I might not have broken my heart again, too. But no.

After I received the ghastly news from my agent that *Blonde Lace* had been consumed in the fire, I felt an urgent desire to see how Reuben was coping with his loss. I bathed and changed into a simple dark Schiaparelli suitable for the surreal atmosphere of a studio in ruins. I then drove back at top speed. The entire place reeked of smoke and burned dreams.

Grim-faced accountants trudged out of Reuben's office before Miss Hardy admitted me. As she closed the door, Reuben advised Miss Hardy to go home. When she protested that she would wait until he was done, Reuben said he expected to spend the night working in his office.

The sweat-soaked tiger of that afternoon had resumed his disguise as a film executive. When had Reuben found time to transform himself into the pin-striped figure I thought I knew so well? Despite his dapper appearance, Reuben looked haggard as he explained Monolithic's crisis. When he spoke of *Blonde Lace,* I detected a faint tremble in his hands.

"My back is to the wall," he confessed to me at last. "How can I keep it all going? How can I pay everyone? I don't know what I am going to do."

The sight of that powerful man reduced to such a piteous state tore at my heart-

Opposite Page: Reuben Lilienthal

strings. "Well, for one thing," I declared, "you can take me off salary for the next few weeks. What's more, I am going to get every star and director and executive on this lot to do the same thing! It's more important that you pay the little people."

Reuben rapidly blinked, his eyes glistening. "You would really do that for me?"

"And more, too, if only you would let me," I said impulsively.

"Madra," he whispered, staring at me as if for the first time, "I could kiss you."

I smiled. "What are you waiting for?" I asked.

An instant later we were locked in a ferocious embrace.

GEORGIA JAMES
From *Hollywood Talks*

You cannot imagine the agony we all felt about *Blonde Lace*. Like losing a child. I was scared that Erik was going to go out of his head with grief. So was Zena.

Then to top it all, we were worried about the studio itself. We all figured Lilienthal would be fired the second the suits arrived from New York, and then where would we all be? Even with another guy in place, where could they find the dough to keep the studio running? A couple of million dollars is peanuts nowadays, but back in 1941 that was major wampum. All of the banks Monolithic had dealings with had turned Lilienthal down flat. There was a sense that they were hoping to sell off the studio's bones for whatever scratch they could get.

Come Thursday morning, I was one tuckered tootsie. My back ached from lugging pails of water. I couldn't use my typewriter from the blisters on my mitts. But I had an appointment that day to talk with Lilienthal about my treatment for *Kept in the Dark*, and I decided to go. Hell or high water—or earthquakes—you kept appointments with the man.

You could have knocked me over with a sneeze when Lilienthal told me to forget about making the movie. I asked what else he had in mind for Gene.

"Not a thing," he said.

"You don't believe this bunk that she's bad luck for us?" I asked. The morning papers had been full of it.

He shrugged. "Maybe I do, maybe I don't," he said. The main thing was that he didn't have the coin to sign Gene to that million-dollar contract. He was going to have to let her go. In fact, Gene was due to arrive any minute to get the word directly from him.

"She'll be all right," he insisted. "Metro wants her, and so does Zanuck."

"But Mono has already become like home to Gene," I said. "She won't want to go anywhere else."

"She's got no choice," he told me. "And neither do I." If somehow the studio survived the current mess, he said, it was going to have to cut back. There wouldn't be enough money to launch a new star like Gene. There wouldn't be money for a lot of things. Including high-priced writers. At that news, I began to worry less about Gene and more for myself.

From *Maharajah of the Movies*

They went for a walk together. Past the imposing row of soundstages. Past the area devastated by the fire. Lilienthal talked to Gene Marshall of Monolithic's earliest days.

He had seen many stars walk along this street over the last twenty years. Beautiful and talented people, most of them. Others simply beautiful, whose fame faded with their charms. There were the people crushed by the talkies, and the personalities lost in changing tastes. The stars who ruined themselves. A few ruined by studio mismanagement. Names spilled from his lips in a rush of memories. Gish. Bow. Keaton. Swanson. Valentino. He sighed deeply when he mentioned Ida Best and the last time he ever saw her, right on that very spot, sporting a sailor hat, waving to him as she hurried for the front gate in 1929.

Then the stars of the thirties. Lombard. Cooper. Tracy. Lord. The good pictures and the bad ones. His years of unparalleled success.

And now today. Bad judgment. Even worse luck. Lilienthal doubted whether he'd be able to hang on to the studio. What he regretted most was that he could no longer be part of Marshall's career. He believed she would become one of the brightest stars of them all.

Marshall said she was willing to take lesser terms. Lilienthal advised her to wait until next week before making such an offer. The odds were that others would be in charge of the studio then, and her lawyer could negotiate with them.

"I'm just sorry we lost your baby picture," he told her. "It was a beauty, believe me."

IVY JORDAN

When Gene asked to borrow my car, I said I was about to use it to visit poor Vicky Steiner at the hospital. She said she needed to get to Pasadena.

"Thinking about getting married?" I asked.

Gene said she was thinking about something else. Then she disappeared to get a car from someone else, I guessed.

Vicky was finally conscious, but said she didn't want to live anymore after hearing about *Blonde Lace.* She blamed herself. The lab never kept all the footage for a film in one spot, but they were doing such a rush job of editing that all of the pieces of *Blonde Lace* just happened to be there. Vicky had only returned from an early lunch when the ceiling suddenly fell in on her, and that was all she knew. Vicky sobbed that her new Oscar was lost in the fire, too.

Gene was back by early evening. Paul drove her. Somehow she had managed to hitchhike her way to Pasadena. Yeah, those were different times, brother! Paul didn't stay long. Gene gave him a quick kiss and sent him away.

What's going on? I wondered.

Gene told me she had decided to hunt up some financial help for Lilienthal, and who knew more about money than Paul's father?

And?

Mr. Ames first wanted to know what was going on with Paul. He said he'd be happy having her for a daughter-in-law, but didn't believe that a domestic life and a Hollywood career went together.

Neither did Gene. Marriage was out of the question for the next few years. She was fond of Paul, she admitted, but had decided to try for stardom in the movies, which was why she had come to call.

Mr. Ames, it seemed, knew more about Monolithic than Gene had supposed. One of his banker chums had loaned money to the studio. So he had a good idea of its financial problems. He also had turned into an admirer of Rubi when they negotiated Gene's contract together.

Gene wondered whether Mr. Ames might have some other banker friends who could advance the studio the huge sums it needed. "Maybe I do," he said. He believed Monolithic to be basically sound despite its crisis. He was busily telephoning around to his associates when Paul took her home.

Wasn't that wonderful?

And Paul?

Gene's excited smile dimmed. She really did like Paul. An awful lot, actually. But they both had other things to do with their lives. He was still in college, with two years of law school afterward. As for herself, well, Gene was determined to make movies. For Monolithic. She'd play second banana to the Bratzanjammer Boys if she had to. But only if Lilienthal still ran the operation.

ERIK VON STERNBERG

From *Eye for Beauty*

Terrible blackness consumed me utterly. The color of ashes.

Somehow late Friday afternoon, I made my way to the studio. I stared again into the pit where *Blonde Lace* was consumed and contemplated the vanity of my vocation. Film was supposed to last forever.

Reuben had summoned me. In his conference room sat Gene and Edward Ames with some gentlemen I did not know. Miss Hardy identified several as members of the studio's New York directors. Ames introduced the rest as a group of bankers. Distinguished blue-chip bankers, as I gathered from their conservative appearance.

The atmosphere was serious, but scarcely as funereal as I expected.

Gene wore powder blue. She smiled at me and squeezed my hand as I sat down next to her. Reuben and Ames explained the reason for the meeting. Ames had assembled a number of financial institutions that would loan Monolithic the money it needed on two conditions.

One, that Lilienthal would remain as head of production. "With certain fiscal restrains," Ames added. Secondly, that Gene would be contracted to star in three films to be made over the next year.

Would I consent to direct her next picture, whatever that might be?

"Gentlemen," I declared. "There's nothing else I would rather do than direct each and every one of Gene's films."

Did I see a sudden shadow of doubt cloud her eyes? But others were talking to Gene, and she turned away.

"We'll deal with your contract later, Miss Marshall," said Ames. "Although you shouldn't expect to get the same sweetheart deal your old lawyer negotiated for you."

Gene smiled and the mood in the conference room suddenly grew cheerful. Georgia showed up, thrilled by the good news, talking very loud and fast about making a musical for Gene with a Navy theme. I half-listened to her and began to imagine my own possibilities.

Gene as a gangster's moll? Gene as a love-struck princess? Gene as a—?

Miss Hardy opened the bar. The New York contingent turned out to be a congenial bunch of cutthroats who got along surprisingly well with the old Pasadena crowd. One banker remarked how everyone's fortunes had come from gold prospecting a century before and there was still a wildcat vein of daring in them all. Besides, said another, America was soon going to need all the entertainment it could get. Movies would be good business in wartime.

Madra arrived, and I was puzzled to notice how affectionate she was with Reuben. I had never seen Madra actually touch him before, but now she kept brushing by him like a cat. She was as gracious as I'd ever seen, turning on the legendary Lord luster for every moneyman in the room. Reuben looked on fondly, almost possessively. Gene herself was no slouch in the charm department, of course, making many an old shark and Ivy Leaguer wish he'd stayed in fighting trim.

For a moment, I wondered whether I was still unconscious at home dreaming all this.

Harry Hale
From ASF's Oral History Project

It was a completely unexpected coup, and everybody was so thrilled about the future we forgot about the last few days' mess. Wanting to show off the studio's great potential to our new benefactors, Lilienthal had us arrange a screening of some rushes from our other pictures in production. There was the new Marsha Hunt, and the Bratzanjammers' *Cracked Ice,* and I forget what else. We also had a bunch of the latest Minky Doodle Dandy cartoons.

When everyone finally got resettled with their drinks in the screening room, the boss said we could all use some laughs to start so let's show a Minky first.

The room went dark, and the screen lit up. But it wasn't Minky Doodle Dandy fluffing his tail like we expected.

Instead, it was Gene Marshall on that nightclub staircase, dancing in a spotlight.

14

Fade Out

CORA HARPER

From *Non-Stop Hollywood* syndicated column

Los Angeles Ledger

NON-STOP HOLLYWOOD

HOLLYWOOD HAS TALKED OF NOTHING ELSE for weeks. "Blonde Lace"—back from the ashes.

A miracle? A mad publicity stunt? We may never learn the truth.

As for me, I'm all for the miracle. I believe in happy endings. That's what makes Hollywood "Hollywood."

Just a few weeks ago, Monolithic Pic-tures was a smoldering pile of despera-tion and debt. Now it rises again, grander than ever. Perhaps they should switch the studio's trademark panther to a phoenix!

Tops among Monolithic's agenda is Gene Marshall, set to star in a trio of pic-tures created especially for her talents. Beginning shooting in September is "Rich Girl," a screwball comedy about a headstrong heiress. Cary Grant is being wooed by Erik von Sternberg to costar.

Backed by a powerful financial combine headed by Edward Ames, studio president Reuben Lilienthal is readying a slate of Christmas releases: Madra Lord and Paul Muni in "Bride of Glory." Trent Osborn and Loretta Young in "Love Me Tomorrow." Ivy Jordan with George Burns and Gracie Allen in "Which Wife?" Other stars visiting the lot soon include Greer Garson, Robert Montgomery, Bing Crosby, Carmen Miranda, and John Payne.

Meanwhile, plans go forward for the simultaneous New York and Hollywood premieres of "Blonde Lace," and I can't begin to describe the tremendous envy this film has aroused from industry insiders who have privately screened it. Madra Lord graces the Chinese Theater festivities here on the arm of the studio president. In New York, Gene Marshall will launch the gala screening at the Regency Theater. It's the very same spot where I discovered Gene only a few fleeting months ago. Of course, I'll be there to cover it!

Heavens, so much has happened since!

A little green birdie tells me that Gene quietly slipped out of town yesterday, bound for a summer in Connecticut with her darling parents. Although she has left behind a handsome Pasadena aristocrat with a sprained heart, Hollywood's croquet-playing elite are relieved.

From *Hollywood Gomorrah*

Police were finally stymied when their laboratory reports on the cans of film proved inconclusive. Any paper trail at the studio relating to the transport of the *Blonde Lace* print after its final preview was lost in the blaze that consumed the postproduction facilities. A number of stars, staff, and studio workers were interviewed, and animator Clifton Davis was even held overnight for questioning, but no one ever admitted any connection with the film's mysterious recovery.

After the police investigation revealed nothing, the studio made no further attempts to find out how the missing film materialized in its executive screening room. "I'm not going to question God's grace," declared Lilienthal.

The ecstatic reception *Blonde Lace* eventually received from the critics, and its huge success with the public, buried any rumors that its disappearance was a publicity stunt meant to bolster business for a weak film. But speculation has never ceased to this day about the true location of the film at the time of the earthquake and fire and where it might have been for three days before its reappearance at Monolithic.

HARRY HALE
From ASF's Oral History Project

Sure, I know what people have said over the years. But, sorry, I'm not bright enough to dream up a screwy stunt like making off with *Blonde Lace* and stashing it somewhere while my office was burning down. Nope, I don't know how that print survived.

It was a dupe we used for the sneak preview the night before the quake. I guess it simply never got back to the editing rooms afterward. Coming back from lunch next day, Vicky assumed that the dupe was there in the lab with the master print and everything else. Evidently it wasn't.

Maybe it was still parked outside the lab in one of our studio vans. It could have been in the dumbwaiter waiting to be taken upstairs. Yes, and as people have speculated since, it might have been in the publicity building.

I admit it's true that sometimes we held on to the preview copy. Not that night, I swear.

Nobody knows how—or if—that print came back to the studio after the preview. It was one of those oddball but-I-thought-you-had-it situations we never figured out afterward. For all I know, it could have been stashed in the trunk of Erik's car.

How it finally wound up in the boss's private screening room is beyond me. Maybe it was mistakenly dropped off there in the first place after the preview. But I guess that wouldn't explain why the reels were in cans marked as Minky Doodle Dandy cartoons. The police dusted them for prints, but they were clean of everything but the projectionist's fingers.

Well, remember, a lot of things at the studio were moved around in a big hurry during the fire. Plenty of valuables waltzed off that day. Some items never found their way back. The dupe could just as easily have been taken by one of the secretaries or grips who didn't know what they had in the back of a van with other stuff. Maybe they panicked once they realized what they had after the news broke so big about the film's loss, and somehow they were able to sneak it back onto the lot later.

I tell you in all honesty, though, it wasn't a publicity stunt. Oh, no, I would never have put everybody through such suffering just for the sake of some headlines. What kind of a guy do you think I am?

GEORGIA JAMES
From *Hollywood Talks*

Jumping Jerusalem, when everyone came to realize that *Blonde Lace* was there on-screen and the entire rest of the film was safe in the projection room as well, we all carried on like it was the Easter story with the original cast. Such hugging, kissing, and screaming like you never saw.

Right then and there, the boss ordered the best postproduction experts in town to take charge. Striking copies for distribution off a print was mighty tricky business. But Vicky and those guys did wonders. Luckily, it all worked in the picture's favor, blending the footage from all the different approaches into a consistent visual texture. That weird glimmering darkness the *Cahiers du Cinéma* crowd loves to go on about? Well, let's just call it a happy accident. However it worked out, that shadowy, smoky look of *Blonde Lace* set the style for all film noir to come.

As far as the miraculous recovery goes, I haven't a clue. The print's whereabouts after the preview remains a mystery right alongside Thelma Todd's murder. It was a

last-minute decision to sneak it out in Riverside, so some of us weren't even there. Afterward, did the film go back with Vicky's crew? They all denied it. Everybody knew zilch. Funny, you'd think somebody would remember having something so bulky as ten reels of feature film.

Some folks believe Madra may have knowingly or not rescued the reels with everything else she hauled out of the publicity building. But I can't imagine she ever got her claws on them. If she had, that movie would've been history. Unless Madra screened it somehow and realized how terrific she came off. But no, her animosity for Gene was too strong. Of course, just then Madra was in the hearts and flowers stage of that screwy fling she had with Lilienthal, so you'd have to throw that into the pot. Still, even if she wanted to, Madra couldn't have smuggled the movie into the screening room all by herself. Not with her bum foot. Somebody must have helped her—but who?

Apart from Miss Hardy—who hated Madra's guts—the only person other than Lilienthal himself who had the complete run of the studio was Harry, I suppose. But why would he have made the effort? Harry only helped Harry.

Ivy Jordan

Just in case you're wondering, I always suspected Erik had that print safe at home the whole time. It'd be just like him to keep his own personal copy. Maybe his hysteria those next few days while it was missing was all just a big act. Erik was crazy enough to do anything to make Gene and *Blonde Lace* a must-see with the public. But Georgia always insisted that even Erik wouldn't dare such a thing.

I'm sorry you never got a chance to pump Harry. To his dying day, Harry swore he knew nothing about the print. But that was Harry's way—he played dumb about everything. Trust me, you don't last as long as Harry did in the big-time publicity racket by actually being as vague as he'd like you to believe.

Whatever. I used to kid Gene that she was the one who stole the picture. Well, in a way she did, when the reviews came out.

Before anything else could befall *Blonde Lace,* I insisted that Gene see it. We screened it as soon as another dupe was processed. Gene's reaction? Oh, she was entranced.

Exhausted though everyone at the studio was, we got right back on the assembly line. That's why they called it a dream factory. I was already making *Which Wife?*

when we did the final redubbing on *Blonde Lace*. The next day, escaping the studio's offer of a big send-off, Gene boarded a plane home.

At first Madra made a big stink over how her role had been chopped up. They say Civil Defense patterned their air raid sirens from the way Madra screamed. But she shut up once all the congratulations rolled in. A year later, after she won the Academy Award, Madra never ceased gabbing about the challenge of playing that role. Still, I think Madra secretly resented the fact that she scored in the supporting actress category. Supporting other actresses wasn't her style, you know.

ACCOUNT OF MABEL LORKOVIC 1254

May 24 19 41

Pay to the Order of Harry Hale $10,000.00

Ten Thousand — and — 00/100 Dollars

BANK OF LOWER CALIFORNIA
2071 SACRAMENTO BOULEVARD
LOS ANGELES, CALIFORNIA

Memo Consultation Mabel Lorkovic

In 1991, I purchased a crate of books from the estate sale of Harry Hale's effects. The books ranged in subject from well-thumbed copies of Mickey Spillane novels to pristine best-sellers of the mid-1930s through the early 1980s. Many of the volumes went into my permanent library.

Eight years later, in a rush for the airport, I grabbed Harry's copy of the James M. Cain novel <u>Double Indemnity</u> for what I reasoned would be a juicy travel read. I was so right! Tucked inside the book between pages 132 and 133 was this check, uncashed.

It is my theory that this check was payment for his help in secretly returning <u>Blonde Lace</u> to the studio—and for his silence afterwards. I also believe that Harry never cashed the check from "Mabel Lorkovic" (see page 186) in order to keep the upper hand in his professional relationship with a certain temperamental film star. Miss Lord declined comment. —Mel

ERIK VON STERNBERG

From *Eye for Beauty*

Some matters are better left a mystery.

The simplest explanation is that the preview print of *Blonde Lace* had been delivered to the executive screening room on the morning of the earthquake and sat there unnoticed through all of our woes. The wrong labels on the cans? No doubt a careless mix-up. Such things often happened.

Of course, the baroque fantasies that individuals subsequently conjured over the years have been a great source of amusement to me. But in the end, they only add to the legend of *Blonde Lace*. It simply proves my point that the public almost always prefers illusion over drab reality.

MONOLITHIC

Today

I am often asked if Gene Marshall gets involved in the day-to-day development of the Gene Doll Collection by Ashton-Drake Galleries. To be very honest, no; but Mel Odom and I talk several times a day in order to get the dolls and her costumes just right.

When working on a new design I always wonder what Gene, the legend of the silver screen, will think about the creation that she has inspired. I have never met Miss Marshall in person, but the doll is as real to me as many of the people I know. While art directing a photo shoot, I have even been known to ask the doll to move a little this way or that. From the second I read Mel Odom's account of Gene Marshall, I was drawn in. She pulls at my heart—the dreamer, and the artist. Gene Marshall is all about the best of the Golden Age of Hollywood, a time when a starlet was groomed, costumed, and guarded by the studios.

Sometimes I send off a note to Gene or Mel, "How is this skirt or that cape? Tell me more about that movie." A quick faxed note might offer suggestions, but her usual style is a box of creamy white gardenias for my office, or a bunch of violets packed in soft green moss will be waiting by my front door at the end of a long day. The sentiments are always thoughtful, "Thank-you for caring so much about the details . . . . GM." When Miss Marshall gives her nod, my heart smiles.

Day after day new costumes and ideas find their way to the drawing board. We are the keepers of a great tradition. Sharing her dream is enough to inspire a whole team of people to work at making the doll special.

It would be an honor to show you the Gene Collection. Write me at Ashton-Drake, 9333 N. Milwaukee Ave., Niles, IL 60714 or call 1-888-FOR-GENE. You can also contact us through the website at www. collectiblestoday.com.

—JOAN GREENE
DIRECTOR
GENE GROUP/*Ashton-Drake Galleries*

Additional Credits

Additional characters created by MARIANNE CLARKSON
Sets by ROBERTO DE CASTRO
Costumes for Miss Marshall by DOLLY CIPPOLA, LYNN DAY,
DOUG JAMES, and TIM KENNEDY
Good-bye New York corsage from Rosalie Purvis
Hair styles for Miss Marshall by SCOTT BODIE, PATTI HOJNACKI, and LAURA MEISNER
Gene's stand-in: CHEECHEE HALL
Gene lettering: BARRY ZAID

PROJECT PRODUCED BY BTD/Beth Tondreau Design, Inc., and STAR BLUE STUDIO, Inc.

FOR BTD
Project management: KIMBERLY JOHNSTON
Design, fakesimile art and design: DANIEL RODNEY
Art direction and design: BETH TONDREAU

Editorial services: K&N BOOKWORKS, INC.

Assistant to Steven Mays: Jamie Havenar

FOR HYPERION

Editor: WILL SCHWALBE
Production director: LINDA PRATHER
Assistant editor: MARK CHAIT

Michael Sommers and Mel Odom respectively thank
Charlie Siedenburg and Charlie Saputo for their loving patience with us.

Special thanks to legal counsel Albert Gottesman, Steven Borell, Edward Davis,
Mitchell Douglas, and Andrew Berger for playing nice.

Paper dolls painted by Judy Johnson copyright © 1999 Ashton-Drake Galleries
All major characters in this book are fictitious. No animals have been harmed during the making of this book.